KNOCK ON ANY
– THE DOOR O

To Paul and Ann
with best
wishes
from Peter

Knock On Any Door
– The Door Opens

Peter Finnigan

The Pentland Press Ltd
Edinburgh · Cambridge · Durham · USA

© Peter Finnigan 1999

First published in 1999 by
The Pentland Press Ltd.
1 Hutton Close
South Church
Bishop Auckland
Durham

British Library Cataloguing in Publication Data.
A catalogue record for this book is available
from the British Library.

ISBN 1 85821 648 6

Typeset by George Wishart & Associates, Whitley Bay.
Printed and bound by Antony Rowe Ltd., Chippenham.

*To my wife, Lavinia
and to Brian and Reuben*

The Author in his early twenties.

When I was 17, it was a very good year.
    A very good year for small time
Girls and soft summer nights.
    We'd head for the lights
On the Village Green
    When I was seventeen.

When I was 21 it was a very good year.
    It was a very good year for city girls
Who lived up the stair
    With all that perfect hair
And it came undone
    When I was 21.

When I was 30 it was a very good year
    It was a very good year
For girls of independent means.
    We'd ride in limousines
Their chauffeurs would drive,
    When I was 35.

But now the days are short,
    I am in the autumn of my years
And now I think of my life as vintage wine
    From fine old kegs from the brim to the dregs
It pours sweet and clear
    It was a very good year.

Irvin Drake

Acknowledgements

With the approach of the Millennium in my 76th year, I look back on my life and realise that I owe a debt of gratitude to many people. These include my great great-grandfather and his partner, Reuben Farrel, for their entrepreneurial skills, which made Finnigans possible. Also composers of popular music such as George Gershwin (who, just like Mozart, died far too young), Irving Berlin and Cole Porter, whose music helped me through my darkest hours, along with such performers as Nat King Cole, Bing Crosby, Frank Sinatra and Cleo Lane.

I should also include Alice Duer Miller, the writer of a book of poems from which the well-known song, 'The White Cliffs of Dover' was taken. They say that there is no more lonely place than a big city. The same applied to a warship with a crew of nearly 2,000. This book provided me with some cultural comfort during the two years of my service abroad. I particularly remember reading the poems aloud with a shipmate during the hot tropical nights on the upper deck of the *Warspite* while swinging round the buoy in Mombasa, waiting for the Japanese Fleet (fortunately it was conspicuous by its absence). Alice's book brought us closer to home and I am grateful for it.

I had the great pleasure of serving with Captain Packer in H.M.S. *Warspite*. His memories, as recorded by his wife Joy in her book, *Deep as the Sea*, have triggered my memories too, particularly of the Battle of Salerno and the Surrender of the Italian Fleet.

There are, of course, many more to whom I am indebted, but I must particularly thank Terry Miller of Corston, the Editor of the *Corstonian*, our village magazine, who encouraged me to write my wartime memoirs and also helped with the preparation of the manuscript of this book. I should also like to acknowledge my indebtedness to the Keepers of the Archives of the Imperial War Museum Picture Library for their renewed permission to publish some of the naval pictures already included in my earlier book, *An Able Seaman's War*, and to thank the Department of Libraries and Theatres, Manchester and the *Manchester Evening News* for the pictures of Finnigans' Department Stores in Market Street and Deansgate, Manchester and Wilmslow on the front cover. I would also like to thank the *Wilmslow Advertiser* for much of the material of the Finnigans' family history contained in the prologue to this book. It was once published in an article of theirs entitled 'From Sailing Ship to Superstore'.

Finally, the most heartfelt thankyou of all goes to my wife Lavinia, without whose support this book would not have been written.

Contents

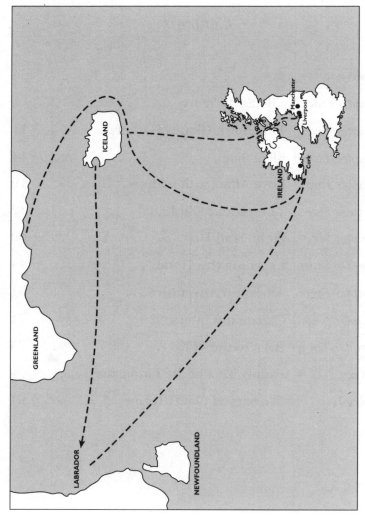

Probable Voyages of Brian Finnigan and Reuben Farrel.

Prologue

It is a far cry from the rigours of an Arctic sailing ship to the smooth sophistication of a speciality department store with a name and reputation known throughout the world

In 1800, unlike today, whale and seal hunting was not frowned upon and many brave seafarers made a good living out of collecting and either making up leather goods or selling the skins to manufacturers. My great great grandfather was one of the former. An Irishman proudly claiming descent from Brian Boru, ancient King of Ireland, he spent summer months sailing off the coast of Newfoundland with fellow Irishman Reuben Farrel who collected animal skins which he made into bags and trunks. These were very much in demand by travellers who needed durable and weatherproof luggage for the long and tedious journeys, in those days by open coach. His success led Reuben to 'swallow the anchor' and set up in business in Liverpool making leather goods. Brian Finnigan, looking for a less arduous future for his son William, decided to apprentice him to Farrel in 1805.

At the time the cotton industry was booming and Manchester was developing into a prosperous city so William and Reuben decided to move there and opened a factory in Salford. Later Brian branched out on his own with a workshop in Newton Mill and a shop in

Market Street, then Manchester's most fashionable area. Thus in 1830 Finnigans was established, and soon won a remarkable reputation all over the North and later in London for high quality leatherware and saddlery.

The opening of the shop coincided with the beginning of the Liverpool Railway and Stephenson's Rocket, the first proper railway in the world, which increased demand for travelling bags and had a highly beneficial effect on William Finnigan's future. It led him to produce specialities like his 'Lady's Train Case', with a special tray for jewellery and enough room for slippers, toiletries and all the paraphernalia vital for a woman's well-being on a long journey and his elaborate Wicker Picnic Basket, which was snapped up not only by English travellers, but also by wealthy Indian Rajahs who ordered it by the dozen to strap on the backs of elephants on safari.

In 1851 Brian took a stand at Prince Albert's Great Exhibition at the Crystal Palace, winning a gold medal for excellence in craftsmanship, thereby spreading Finnigans' reputation even wider. But it was not until 1879 that his son William opened a shop in New Bond Street, London. Soon American millionaires such as the Rockefellers, the Vanderbilts and the Fords joined the Indian Rajahs as customers.

That other famous name, Aspreys, had a shop in Bond Street opposite Finnigans and this created a friendly rivalry between the two merchants. By now, although still specialising in leather and saddlery, Finnigans was also selling clocks and watches, military brushes, silverware and glass and china. My Uncle William told the story of the day he stopped the traffic in Bond Street as he greeted an Indian Rajah and ushered him into Finnigans, where he proceeded to sell him an elaborate fitted dressing-case with brushes, combs and mirrors covered in diamonds and other precious stones. When the shop in Market Street, Manchester became too small for them, Finnigans moved to a more spacious building in Deansgate. With Kendal Milnes at one end and Finnigans at the other, Deansgate became quite a shopping centre. With the space available Finnigans were able to increase their range of merchandise to include a Sports Department, Fashion and Men's Wear as well as Cosmetics and eventually Hardware and T.V. when it was first introduced.

In 1938 Brian took over as Managing Director based in Deansgate and during the War Finnigans contributed to the war effort with the factory producing much-needed webbing equipment for the services. Finnigans was by now as much an ornament to the city as the Town Hall, Rylands Library and Cheethams Hospital. Unlike his predecessors who had been mainly influenced by the Continent, Brian found inspiration in the U.S.A. and built up an export market in New York, Canada and the Caribbean.

After the War, with four and a half years of service in the Navy behind me, I joined Brian in Deansgate and was sent to the States to work at Macys in New York and to help with the furtherance of our export activities. Brian had visited the United States before the War and both of us studied the successful trend of moving city stores to out-of-town locations.

In the 1950s the lease on the Deansgate store was due to expire and we were faced with the choice of moving to some other part of the city or moving into the suburbs. Having found what we considered to be an ideal location in Wilmslow just twelve miles from the City Centre, we moved there. It was a new 'first' for Finnigans but the biggest gamble in history. Fortunately it was a triumphant success – so much so that many other shops followed, making the erstwhile village of Wilmslow into a thriving New Town.

Because I believe we can all learn from previous generations, I have started this narrative with a history. Sadly Finnigans is no more, having suffered the fate of so many family businesses. As you will see, I have dedicated this volume to Brian and Reuben. I would have loved to have met them. I knew Reuben's grandson in the factory in Salford – a great craftsman and teacher. They say that we should always look forward, but it is essential to be aware of our past. With hindsight, perhaps Finnigans might still be going strong but it is no good feeling sad. This book should explain why for me there was life after Finnigans.

CHAPTER ONE

The Early Years

Born on August 27th 1923 in Altrincham, Cheshire (now Greater Manchester), I have failed to display any of the characteristics of the true Virgo who, according to astrologers, is meant to be careful, orderly, efficient, modest, practical and tidy. I feel that I may have strayed in from the next sign, Leo, as those born under this sign are described as strong-willed, energetic and generous. They like colourful and showy things and are attracted to such fields as the theatre (also sales situations). Leos can sometimes be too proud. I was born with a silver spoon in my mouth and you all know what can happen to silver. It can tarnish, but can be re-polished, providing we are prepared to make the effort.

Because she died when I was nine months old, I never knew my mother. According to her Death Certificate she died of gangrene of the lung and pneumonia while in Edinburgh. There is a mystery surrounding her death as we could not understand what she was doing in Edinburgh or how she had contracted such a dreadful disease. Today, with the advent of penicillin and antibiotics, gangrene of the lung is virtually unknown.

My father had very good taste; Marjorie Mason was an attractive twenty-three-year-old. She was the daughter of a local greengrocer and her parents did not approve of the match because of the age difference; my father was over 40. This would not concern anybody today. It was good to mix the bloods of a third-generation Irishman and an English girl. This could account for my gregarious nature.

I was brought up by my father and a series of governesses. Because of the eight-year age-gap between my sister Pam and myself, I felt more like an only child. My various governesses included a lady called Deeney, who spoiled me, Miss Crosland, whom I really disliked, and Miss Amor (Cecile), who eventually became my step-mother. More about her later.

Mine was a mainly happy childhood, although, as a loner, I tended to be teased at school. At the age of five I was sent to Loreto Convent, only five minutes from home. When I eventually left, I was one of the oldest boys in the school and I made my first Communion surrounded by attractive young ladies. I had a special crush on a particular girl called Peta, who was only six at the time. Even at that age, I revelled in the company of the opposite sex. Greta Gynt, a film star of the fifties, was also a pupil at Loreto Convent.

I was obviously destined for the Navy from an early age, as I wore a sailor suit almost as soon as I could walk. Nevertheless I could hardly wait to get into normal clothes like most of the other boys. Altrincham, Cheshire (now Greater Manchester) was a dormitory town for Manchester, where Finnigans had an exclusive department store (See Prologue). 'Tree Oaks', named after the massive tree in the garden, was a rambling old house with enough rooms for the whole family – myself, Dad, Pam, and my governess of the time, as well as a retinue of servants including a cook, a parlour maid, 'tweeny' and the butler, who was called 'Dainty'. Our large garden allowed us to have great fun with our friends, as well as providing paths for circling on our bicycles and for the two ponies, 'Sunshine' and 'Princess' often ridden bareback. Riding was one of my father's favourite activities and he had two horses, Jemly, a magnificent Arab, and Manley, a chestnut. He rode to hounds with the North Cheshire Hunt and I often accompanied him on Sunshine. She was a great hunting pony and we enjoyed galloping across the Cheshire countryside. Once I fell off at a jump and Sunshine made sure that she did not tread on me, for which I was truly grateful. Because Pam and I were often forced to ride when we would rather have been doing something else, we did not grow up with a love of the sport. My daughter Caroline, however, has taken after her grandfather and rides at every opportunity. In those days it was customary for the youngest rider in at the kill to be 'blooded' (with the fox's blood) or to be given the mask (the fox's head). At the time I was proud to be honoured in this way, although I am sure that today the practice would be condemned by the anti-hunting lobby.

My musical education began with listening to such artistes as Rudy Vallee and Bing Crosby on the radio. I also used to buy their records and those of the Big Bands, led by such notables as Artie Shaw, Fats Waller and Benny Goodman. I grew up in what was probably the greatest ever era for popular music. Not only did I see every film that Bing and Fred Astaire ever made, but I managed to catch up with the best of the Hollywood films, most of which have been revived for T.V. today. The back row of the stalls in the 'one-and-nines' with your favourite girl was a wonderful place to dream. I devoured film magazines such as *Picturegoer* and *Film Weekly*, regularly falling in love with glamorous stars such as Lana Turner and youngsters such as Deanna Durbin and Judy Garland. Deanna, incidentally, hailed from Manchester – a true case of 'local girl making good'.

I was sent to dancing class at an early age, where I joined a group of attractive young ladies. Ever since dancing school days I have enjoyed the terpsichorean art (I even served on a Destroyer called the *Terpsichore* during the War), fancying myself as a budding Astaire or Gene Kelly. I have kept up my tap dancing, and even today I am always prepared to get up and perform. In those days, there were numerous formal parties, many of them given by friends and often at the Assembly Rooms in Bowdon. It was customary at such parties for a young lady to enter the names of her partners for each dance on a card specially designed for the purpose. I am glad to say that I was usually included. I felt sorry for the lonely young men left off the list, often because they could not dance.

As well as horse-riding, I enjoyed tennis and skiing and in the winter was often taken to St Cergue in Switzerland, where I attained my Bronze medal for dashing down a slope on skis without falling over. One year (I was about nine at the time) I fell hopelessly in

Herbert on Manley.

Cecile Amor on Sunshine.

Peter, Herbert and Pam in the garden at Tree Oaks.

Wonderful sit-up-and-beg Rolls Royce with Herbert, Pam and Peter.

Cecile Amor at Hardelot – note the beach pyjamas.

Peter on Sunshine.

Four of the eight houses remaining in Hardelot after the War.

love with a young girl of ten at our hotel. Unfortunately my love was not reciprocated and I cried all the way back to England in the train.

The first holidays that really registered with me, as a child of five, was our visit to Hardelot, near Le Touquet, on the Channel coast in northern France. For years most of the Finnigan family spent the summer holidays there, including Dad and Pam, Uncle Charlie, Uncle Bernard, Auntie Allie and my cousin Barney and Brian and Daphne (see Index I, Family Tree.) I remember the sand, sun and rolling dunes and the super group of children we met there of all nationalities. Sand-sailing was all the rage and we had great fun joining in the 'keep fit' classes with the adults and children. Le Touquet had a thriving Casino and I know my Dad enjoyed the odd flutter now and again. Auntie Allie, wife of Bernard, one of Father's brothers, arranged for a governess to meet us in France. Her name was Cecile Amor. She was 21 and very 'green'. She was a remarkable young lady who managed to cope with a spoiled six-year-old in a foreign country and thereafter in a large house in Cheshire. I will always be grateful for her constant support in my battles with my father. These could have had something to do with the generation gap, and Cecile was the diplomat in the family. She loved singing and playing the piano and was undoubtedly responsible for encouraging my love of music. Being half French, she helped me to learn the language, something that proved essential when I spent time in Switzerland as part of my training. Cecile was destined to have a great influence on my life and she also nursed Dad through his cancer and became his wife in his latter years. She too died of the dreaded cancer, as did many members of my family. There can be no question of heredity because each of them died of a different type.

Those who have seen Jacques Tati in *M. Hulot's Holiday* will realise what sort of resort Hardelot was in the thirties. The first golf course, The Pines, was built in 1932, and when I re-visited Hardelot in 1996, I had the pleasure of playing there and also on another golf course which was built later called The Dunes. It is interesting to see that only eight of the original buildings survived the bombings by the R.A.F. during the War. (See picture p. 5.) Another pastime, sand yachting, is still popular over there and I have been invited to the centenary celebrations which will take place in 2006. God willing, I hope to attend. I found out that the first ninety years had recently been celebrated and that the guests of honour included Prince Edward and the grand-daughter of Blériot, the famous flyer. I learned later that Father was rather keen on Blériot's daughter, whose visit coincided with our own.

Auntie Gertrude, wife of William (see Family Tree, Index I), had a cottage in Aldeburgh on the beautiful Suffolk coast, now famous for its music festival at the Maltings in Snape, and we stayed with her on numerous occasions. The boating lake at nearby Thorpeness became the Spanish Main to us children. It was no more than three feet deep, so we could sail and row quite safely among the islands, occasionally landing to attack the Pirate Chiefs, dragons and the like, which we met around every corner. Imagination played a wonderful part in my childhood and I cannot understand why today's parents spend so much money on toys, which are often broken before Christmas or the birthday is over.

Aldeburgh was a popular sailing centre and I enjoyed crewing on a very large yacht on the River Alde; a highlight of the holiday was the annual Regatta with the great splash of colour provided by the sails of the dinghies as they struggled to win the coveted cup. In Aldeburgh we carried out gang warfare with the local lads – they always seemed to be better armed than the visitors – and one day I avoided being hit on the head by one of their staves only by jumping over our fence like an Olympic high jumper. These were happy days, and although the storm clouds were gathering, we had no idea of the cataclysmic events that were to follow this period of calm.

Like many Mancunians, we used the North Wales coast as one of our main holiday venues. The Finnigan family had lived in Colwyn Bay, and we ended up buying a cottage in Rhos-on-Sea, where Cecile came to live after my father died. The Grand Hotel in Llandudno has great memories for me. I particularly recall meeting two eleven-year-old twin girls who caused double trouble for a pal and myself, as we could never tell one from t'other. I attended Rhos-on-Sea School, where I boarded for a while before going on to Stonyhurst College. We swam in the local unheated baths most mornings even in the winter. We really must have been tough in those days. My second wife Lavinia and I visited Llandudno a few years ago and we felt that it had managed to retain its Victorian watering place charm. Unfortunately the era of the Grand Hotel is over and the one in Llandudno has been taken over by a holiday company and spoilt out of all recognition.

Teenage Plus

At the age of thirteen I was sent to Stonyhurst College to be educated by the Jesuits, known as 'the black spies' by us young reprobates. In retrospect, I believe they were good teachers. Having said that, we gave them a hell of a time, particularly in my first year. Although I had easily passed my Common Entrance from Rhos-on-Sea School, I was not particularly academic. Stonyhurst is one of the major Catholic schools in this country and the buildings date back to the sixteenth century, just after the Reformation. Because on my first day, when asked my name, I gave my number too, I was always known as Peter Finnigan 102.

My time at Stonyhurst was like the Curate's Egg. I did not excel myself either in the classroom or on the sports field. I played a little golf and rugger every Saturday afternoon, whatever the weather. I was beaten on occasion with a ferule, horrifying to today's parents, but it did not seem to do me any harm – or good for that matter. I also took part in exercises with the Officers Training Corps and, before I left, managed to pass my School Certificate and to Matriculate – the equivalent of six specific G.C.S.E.s today. I feel that despite the good teaching of the Jesuits, music and painting were somewhat neglected, and that greater emphasis on these would have opened up artistic opportunities to us which we missed. The buildings contained many valuable paintings and art treasures but these failed to make any great impact on the artistic sensibilities of the pupils. As for history, whereas nowadays modern history is taught as part of the national curriculum, in those days at Stonyhurst the period mainly covered was ancient and medieval history from the Romans to Henry VIII.

I left Stonyhurst at sixteen and started work in Manchester as a clerk in the family firm of Finnigans. Believe it or not, I found myself working in an office where the clerks still sat on high stools and used quill pens! Shortly after I left school, war broke out.

CHAPTER TWO

The Storm Clouds Gather

We were aware, of course, of how our parents had fought and, in many cases, died during the First World War, the 'War to end all wars', as they called it. (Little did they know!) We used to shudder at the pictures of the men in the trenches and of the unbelievable slaughter still vivid in the memories of those who had lived through those terrible experiences. But we didn't fully realise how badly Germany had been affected by the War. We knew vaguely about the rise of the Nazi Party and how Hitler had helped the German people to regain their sense of identity, but any awareness of his diabolical treatment of the Jews didn't really percolate through to the average British citizen of the time. In 1939, when Hitler's lust for world domination manifested itself so blatantly in the invasion of Poland, it took many of us by surprise.

When war was declared, in 1939, I was sixteen years of age, and I vividly remember the excitement of the call up, the so-called 'phoney war', when nothing seemed to happen, the evacuation of Dunkirk with the gallant small ships and the abortive Dieppe Raid, the blitz on Manchester and my fire-watching nights at Finnigans' Department Store in Deansgate I also remember the radio programmes on the wireless, such as *It's That Man Again*, with Tommy Handley and *Monday Night at Eight*. These did much to keep our spirits up in the dark days of the war. In 1940 Britain seemed to be alone in Europe in the battle against Nazi tyranny. France was occupied by the Germans, leaving only a small stretch of water between them and us.

The recent D-Day celebrations and the commemoration of V.E. and V.J. Day have brought memories of those eventful wartime years flooding back, and I hope that the reader will enjoy sharing them with me. To the average young person of today, the Second World War is just a part of history. As a young person, I was part of that history.

From Dad's Army to the *Andrew*, 1941–2

As a boy of sixteen, I was determined to make my contribution to the War effort, so I joined the Home Guard, nowadays commonly known as 'Dad's Army' after the well-known T.V. programme still being shown today. We used to meet on most evenings after work at the 'Axe and Cleaver' pub in Dunham Massey, near Bowdon where I was living. Fortunately my time in the Officers' Training Corps at Stonyhurst had made me familiar with the rifle, and we used to keep guard at night just in case the Germans decided to invade, although I did wonder what a group of old men and boys could have done against the Nazi hordes. Fortunately we were never tested, although one night we received a Red Alert. It was rumoured that an invading force had actually manned barges in France, but that the R.A.F. had set fire to the sea, thereby – thank goodness! – preventing them from setting out.

In spite of the military training I had received at school, I was determined not to be called up into the Army. I had always been fascinated by the sea ever since, as a boy of five, I had stood on the deck of the Channel Ferry on the way to France for our holidays and watched the white cliffs of Dover disappear into the mist. Hence, during my period in the Home Guard, I volunteered for the Navy. It was, I believe, a wise choice, since it enabled me to see the world at His Majesty's expense and live to tell the tale. I was only seventeen when I first volunteered, so had to wait a year before setting out on my great adventure. One of the considerations that had influenced me had been that in the Navy I would at least have a bunk to sleep in rather than some muddy old trench. As it happened, I was issued with a hammock, but was not always able to sling it and often had to be satisfied with a mess deck stool or table, and sometimes a locker between decks.

CHAPTER THREE

All at Sea

The Navy had a habit of sending you as far away from home as possible, so it was not surprising that my first destination was Plymouth, a 14-hour journey by train, standing up most of the way as the train was full up with matelots, Wrens and other service personnel returning from leave. From Plymouth I crossed the Tamar to Torpoint and H.M.S. *Raleigh*, where I was to spend the next ten weeks becoming acclimatised to the Navy. This was my initial training and I shared a hut with a very mixed bunch of 'shipmates'. They included boys from the Glasgow Gorbals. It involved some serious soul-searching.

By the time the course was over, a lot of character-building had taken place and we had learned to live with each other. (Perhaps today's young people would benefit from such an experience.) I was a Plymouth Rating – an Ordinary Seaman, later to become an Able Seaman. Not very able and not much of a seaman.

My first 'floating' ship was H.M.S. *Shropshire*, later to be seconded to the Australian Navy as H.M.S. *Canberra*. She was a County Class Cruiser and her task was to escort convoys to all parts of the world, convoys that were desperately vital to our survival and which played their part in the arena of so much death and destruction.

The following are some recollections of my first sea-going experiences in H.M.S. *Shropshire*.

My baptism included scrubbing decks with long handled scrubbers at 0600 hours in all kinds of weather. Never had breakfast tasted so good. Other sea-going duties included 'Captain of the Heads' (looking after the loos) and painting ship's side (and other parts). My watch-keeping included a stint as a 'Look out' on the bridge (four hours on, eight hours off). I kept my eyes skinned for any unusual activity. This was often difficult, particularly when we were rounding the Cape of Good Hope in very rough weather with the massive waves sweeping over the bridge and soaking us to the skin. Because, on occasions I mislaid my wellington boots, I often waded barefoot, ankle deep in water. I never caught a cold and I can only put this down to the therapeutic properties of salt water.

As we approached the Equator, Flying Fish kept popping up ahead of us. It was as if they wanted to lead us safely to port. They obviously appreciated the scraps that the cooks dropped into the sea, although this was really against regulations as enemy ships might have located our position from the food trail.

Our two Walrus reconnaissance sea planes were also great flyers, although it was said that they were so slow that they could wait for the Heinkels and shoot them down as they passed. This story could have been apocryphal; we, at any rate, did not have a chance to prove it. The Walruses were catapulted by steam from their rails on the upper deck (see picture, p. 16) and picked up by the ship's crane when they landed on the sea. One

The County Class Cruiser, H.M.S. Shropshire at speed in the South Atlantic. Her two Walrus aircraft can be clearly seen.

day in Freetown Harbour in West Africa one Walrus sank (apparently the Navigator had forgotten to close the wireless cock and the water had streamed in). The crew jumped into the inflatable dinghy and the Captain was furious; he had to move the ship over to the aircraft, send a diver down to attach the rope from the crane and lift the aircraft on to its 'rails'. 'Jack' had a free front seat for this drama and undoubtedly the Walrus crew was in dead trouble with the Captain when they returned to the ship.

On this trip we were off to Madagascar via Cape Town and Durban, accompanying merchantmen along with the Aircraft Carrier *Illustrious*, which spent most of her time practising take-off and landing techniques. We saw many planes overshoot the deck and finish up in the 'drink'. Fortunately, the pilots were almost always rescued and the planes lifted. One convoy escort duty took us to the Seychelles, which, as it is on the Equator, is one of the hottest places in the world. Sadly, there was no shore leave. The incidence of V.D. among the native population was too high and the will of the average rating too weak.

After a brief period in Simonstown, where we enjoyed diving off the rocks into the Atlantic as well as over the ship's side, we set off in very rough weather around the Cape of Good Hope. When we reached Durban many of the crew, who were South Africans and had not been home for two years, looked forward to spending a few days with their families. This was not to be, at least for the moment, because *Shropshire* was ordered to accompany another convoy back to Simonstown then. The South African ratings registered their displeasure by lining up on the guard rail and barracking whoever came by. These included some soldiers and a Pusser's assistant carrying a suitcase. 'What have you got in that case?' they shouted, much to the embarrassment of the poor old canteen assistant, who could very well have been taking sugar or tea to his friends ashore. It must have been frustrating for the South Africans to see their parents on the other side of the dockyard fence and not be able to join them. Fortunately it was not long before we returned to Durban and the boys got their leave. Personally, I was grateful for the hospitality I received from the O'Reillys in Cape Town and my other friends in Durban. A run ashore in the Cape meant a welcome bath and steak for breakfast. I also enjoyed visiting the local sights in Cape Town and Durban.

Because of my time at Stonyhurst, I was judged to be officer material. Therefore I never reached Madagascar but left the ship in Cape Town to join H.M.S. *Good Hope*, otherwise known as the Seaview Hotel, Port Elizabeth. Although this was not as idyllic as it sounds, I spent the most enjoyable days of my war service there. A tidal swimming pool, a girl called Elsa, and other distractions made it difficult to do otherwise. The idea was to turn me into a Naval Officer but, at the end of the course in the Navigation exam., I steered my ship over Table Mountain and the Examining Officer threatened to resign if I did not fail. Along with three other failures, I was off to Pietermaritzburg on a wonderful, slow, slow train. (So slow that we even stopped at Ladysmith to go to a movie – I remember it well – Bing Crosby in *The Birth of the Blues*.)

CHAPTER FOUR

Love Affair with a Ship Begins – 1942

Pietermaritzburg was merely a transit camp, and before long I was on my way to Durban to join the famous Battleship *Warspite*. Captain Packer, who was commanding her at the time, was a most distinguished officer, and one whom I was proud to serve under. He had started his career as a midshipman in *Warspite*, and now he was her Captain. She was a 'headlines' ship if ever there was one, having taken part in the battle of Narvik, off Norway and also fought at Taranto (when the entire Italian Fleet was effectively put out of action). Our task, this time, was to keep the Japanese Fleet as quiet as possible in the South Atlantic and, along with our sister ship, H.M.S. *Valiant*, and various cruisers and destroyers, we sailed to Mombasa in Kenya. My final recollection of leaving Durban was to watch the figure of Paula Gibbs, known as the Angel of Song, as she serenaded us from the jetty when we left harbour. We all appreciated her lovely voice as the strains of the 'White Cliffs of Dover' gradually faded into the distance. Fortunately for us, the Japanese Fleet stayed in port. Had they not, our World War I battleships would have been no match for their modern, fast ships. However, we did spend many nights in our picket boat, dropping small depth charges along the boom nets that were

Resolution and Warspite in line abreast.

spread across the harbour. This was to deal with any one-man submarines that might be lurking. Even though the depth charges were small, having dropped one, it was 'Full Speed Ahead' to get out of the way of the blast. Thank goodness we never had to drop a big one (as were our orders if we ever saw a submarine) because we'd probably have blown our stern off. After six months of such operations, the *Warspite* was sent back to the U.K., where I had my first leave for 21 months.

While we had been away, things had begun to happen in the Mediterranean. The siege of Malta was coming to an end and plans were afoot for the first invasion of Europe. The *Warspite* was to play her part in all this. After a refit in Gourock and gun trials at Scapa Flow (where the sheep outnumbered the people), we set off for Alexandria in Egypt where we were to await the orders for our participation in 'Operation Husky'. From our berth in the dock at the end of Sister Street, we had to brave the dreaded 'Garry' operators. We were forced to go ashore in pairs as many unsuspecting matelots had got drunk and been led into the winding streets, mugged and robbed. This made going ashore quite hazardous and we were glad to move on to the comparative calm of Malta.

Malta to Italy by Way of Sicily – 1943

By now Rommel had been defeated in North Africa and the Axis forces had been driven out of that continent, so it was logical that the next step would be the invasion of

Sicily and Italy. Preparations were soon underway for 'Operation Husky', described by Admiral of the Fleet Sir Andrew Cunningham as *'The most momentous enterprise of the war, striking for the first time at the enemy in their own land.'*

Warspite and our sister ship, H.M.S. *Valiant*, along with the Aircraft Carrier *Formidable*, were to cover the landing in Sicily, support the army ashore and deal, of course, with the elusive Italian Fleet.

My action station was on the bridge, where I passed on the orders to the 15 inch guns through a voice-pipe. From this vantage point I had a great view of the operation, although the noise of those massive guns was deafening as they dispatched their lethal charges at unimaginable velocity.

To the disgust of everyone, the Italian fleet failed to materialise except, that is, for a few submarines, which were quickly pounced upon by our destroyers. Nevertheless, a U Boat damaged one of our Cruisers and the Aircraft Carrier *Indomitable* was hit by a German aerial torpedo. As a result, we were delegated to escort the *Indomitable* back to Malta.

In Malta, although the siege was over, food was still very scarce, but it came as no surprise that ever-resourceful 'Jack' was able to dig out 'steak, egg and chips' in a local restaurant. This was to be our staple diet and we usually managed to find a source of it wherever we went.

After *Warspite* had arrived with other units of the Mediterranean Fleet, Malta still continued to be bombed by enemy planes based in Sicily and the toe of Italy. Our

Anti-Aircraft guns succeeded in shooting down some of the offending aircraft, eventually dissuading them from their activities. I was delighted to receive a visit from two of my old shipmates from H.M.S. *Good Hope*, who were now officers on Motor Torpedo Boats. I, being a mere Able Seaman while they were officers, it was necessary to borrow some 'civvies' before we could socialise and, thus rigged, we were able to enjoy an evening's dancing beneath the stars with some attractive Maltese lasses.

Malta was a 'fun' place for a run ashore, where the sailors enjoyed frequenting the 'Gut', a notorious area, where additional favours could be obtained from the so-called 'Barbers'. This 'landmark' was pulled down some time after the war ended.

The landing in Sicily had been quite successful and had entailed a minimum of casualties. However, in early July, the advance of the 8th Army was held up at Catania and we were ordered to set sail immediately to bombard the defending troops. With a deadline to meet to commence the onslaught, it was full speed ahead for the 'Old Lady'. This meant twenty knots – tops. We reached twenty-two and a half. The boiler didn't blow up but we jammed our steering gear. Ever since 1914 the *Warspite* had had trouble with her steering and, despite numerous refits, the fault had never been fully corrected. As a result of this jamming we sailed round in a vicious circle and lost a precious ten minutes while a repair was effected. Notwithstanding this set-back, we arrived at Sicily on time and, after being attacked by submarines (quickly dealt with by our destroyers) and enemy aircraft, we carried out a successful bombardment, enabling the army to recapture Catania and, subsequently, the whole island.

Once more we withdrew to Malta, where we received a signal from Admiral Cunningham: *'Operation well executed. When the Old Lady lifts up her skirts she certainly can run.'* We were quite proud that we were the only one of the 'Big Boys' to have blazed at the enemy. From then on the *Warspite* became known as 'The Grand Old Lady'.

Our skipper, Captain Packer, happened to be married to Joy Packer, the famous South African writer, who had many contacts around the world. One of these was Noel Coward, who was visiting Malta to entertain the troops. As a result we were treated to a special showing of his recently completed film, *In Which We Serve*, as well as a sample of his particular brand of humour. I shall never forget the wonderful sound of laughter as we sat under the Mediterranean stars on the upper deck of *Warspite*, thoroughly enjoying this magic respite from wartime routine. We were the only ship to receive a visit from the great man and, as you may imagine, we were the envy of the fleet.

Next came the invasion of the Italian mainland across the narrow Messina Straits. We carried out a bombardment of Reggio and the following day Canadian forces landed virtually unopposed. The 8th Army's long trek up the Italian Peninsula was under way.

The Surrender of the Italian Fleet

'The Italian Fleet now lies at anchor under the guns of the fortress of Malta.'

We had carried out the bombardment of the Italian mainland at Reggio in support of the Canadian landing there and had returned to Malta. We were now sailing at 'full speed ahead' to cover the British and American landings at Salerno. By courtesy of the BBC, Major Glen Miller and his great band were soothing us on our way when: 'We interrupt this broadcast to announce that Italy has surrendered'.

We were 'Force H', the *Warspite* and *Valiant*, together with many other ships. The objective was for the army to reach Naples as soon as possible and, in order to achieve this, it had been decided to land troops at Salerno. We had been delegated to cover the landings and prevent any interference from the enemy. A nice maternal job.

At the announcement of the surrender, there was great excitement on the Mess Deck. The question was how would the Italian Fleet react? Would they scuttle? Would they come over to us? The crew ran a sweepstake on it.

Although Italy had caved in, we did not relax for a moment. Every gun was manned. At 21.30 it started. We were attacked relentlessly by German aircraft with bombs and torpedoes. As they attacked 'up-moon', the clear Mediterranean night was a gift for determined aircraft. They could see us but we couldn't see them, so, at the first sound of a plane's engine, we opened fire with our anti-aircraft guns. They couldn't take it. Of course they continued to drop bombs and fire off torpedoes, but indecisively, and we got so used to these erratic attacks that 'Action Stations' was no longer called. Instead, guns of the duty watch were allowed to engage at will. This enabled us to catch up on some much-needed sleep. Exhausted for lack of it, I found myself a spot on top of a locker between decks and slept through the noise of the guns.

My action station was on the bridge with the Officer of the Watch, a Midshipman and the Captain. As well as passing orders to the 15-inch guns, I acted as lookout for submarines, torpedoes and enemy ships. One particular night I will never forget. Almost incredibly to me, I saw a torpedo heading straight for us, having broken through the barrage. 'Torpedo off the port bow!' I roared. The Captain moved the ship, all 30,600 tons of her, out of the way of it and it slid by harmlessly on the port side. All of us on the bridge heaved such a sigh of relief that it could have been heard on the mainland!

At this time there was an atmosphere of keen expectancy on board, and when we picked up Commander 'Butch' Butcher, General Eisenhower's aide-de-camp, we guessed that something big was in the wind. Sure enough, we were ordered to meet the Italian 'Spezia Fleet' off Cape Bon, N. Africa, and conduct them to Malta. It was 'surrender' and I was one of the lucky ones to profit from the mess deck sweepstake. Meanwhile, German aircraft had sunk the Italian Battleship *Roma*, on the way down from northern Italy, killing the Italian Commander-in-Chief.

Under the guns of the Warspite, the Italian Littorio Class Battleship is seen steaming into Malta, 10th September, 1943.

27

We sighted the Italian Fleet, bows on, at 30,000 yards. There were two 15-inch battleships, five cruisers and nine destroyers. Ships as far as the eye could see. You may imagine what a fine sight they made. At long last, after all the hassle, they were in our hands. We were *Warspite*, *Valiant* and certain Destroyers, including one French and one Greek. We had to be careful not to move our guns as the Italians were somewhat trigger-happy after their experiences on the way. We formed up ahead of them and led them into Grand Harbour in Malta. It was then that Admiral Cunningham sent the famous signal: *'The Italian Battle Fleet now lies at anchor under the guns of the fortress of Malta'*.

The Battle of Salerno

The 'buzz' when we got to Malta was that we would soon be on the way home. We were not able to say goodbye to our island friends because of security – 'Careless Talk' and all that – but, sure enough, 'all hands fall in for leaving harbour' was soon being piped and we were on our way. Would that it had been so simple! The course of events that followed determined that we would not be seeing the U.K. for some time to come.

No sooner had we left harbour than we altered course, and a broadcast by the Captain told us that we were going to Salerno, where the Americans had been pulled back onto the beaches and Admiral Cunningham had requested that the *Warspite* and the *Valiant*, accompanied by an aircraft carrier, should be dispatched post haste to support them.

On the way down, we were once more attacked by German torpedo bombers and, once more, our steering gear jammed, delaying our arrival.

Eventually we sailed into Salerno and what a sight it was that greeted us! From my 'action stations' position on the bridge, a mile off shore, I had a bird's-eye view. There were landing craft and ships everywhere, frantically shunting backwards and forwards to the beach to carry reinforcing supplies and troops from the troop carriers.

The Gunnery Officer told us that the Germans had a secret weapon, called a Glider Bomb, which was dropped from a great height and controlled by radio during its descent. We heard with horror how one had been 'glided' on to the U.S.S. Cruiser *Savannah*, causing great devastation and carnage and killing more than 100 of the crew. We learned later than one had also sunk the Italian Battleship *Roma* after the Italian fleet had surrendered.

In the knowledge of this, we set about our task of preparing for the bombardment. The Captain of Marines went ashore with a Wireless Telegraphist whose job it was to signal back to the ship the ranges for our 15-inch guns. Thus assisted, we succeeded in wiping out a considerable number of German Troops on the other side of the cliffs.

As might be expected, the Germans were not too pleased with us and they sent in *Stuka* dive bombers. These caused more noise than damage and we succeeded in shooting three of them down.

I was one of the few who was able to take breakfast

From over the bows of H.M.S. Illustrious, Warspite entering Grand Harbour in Malta after being damaged by Glider Bombs at Salerno. Seafire on deck of Illustrious.

that morning and, on my return to the bridge, we noticed a tiny speck in the sky that seemed to be growing rapidly bigger. Was this the dreaded Glider Bomb? We were soon to discover that there were three of them!

At a stroke, every Anti-Aircraft gun on the ship opened-up – but to no avail. One of the enemy missiles scored a direct hit amidships in the starboard hangar, which caught fire. (The *Warspite* did not carry Walruses, so the hangars were empty.) Another narrowly missed us but damaged the port side hull and, mercifully, a third fell harmlessly to starboard.

For a few moments there was a stunned silence on the bridge before the Captain ordered the fire-crew into action and attempted to steer the ship further down the coast for the purpose of continuing the bombardment. It was to no avail. The engine room was flooded and we started to drift.

The bomb that landed in the hangar had blown up between decks, letting in water and killing three men on the Stokers' Mess Deck and seven more by the flash passing through the vents of the gun shields. Twenty more men were injured, but the fact that we suffered so few casualties out of a ship's compliment of about 2,000 was nothing short of a minor miracle. Sea water had got into the kit locker flats and some of the crew, including myself, had only the clothes we stood up in – a pair of shorts and a shirt.

So there we were: a sitting target, a mile off shore, out of control and drifting towards a minefield. It quickly became apparent that it was necessary to 'get the hell out of it' as soon as possible.

CHAPTER FIVE

'The Grand Old Lady'

What a hopeless, hapless state of affairs! There was the poor old *Warspite*, drifting helplessly in Salerno Bay, and heading towards a minefield, with the ever-present threat that Jerry would return and finish us off! The Skipper, Captain Packer, had served as a Midshipman on this same ship thirty years before, at the Battle of Jutland, when the *'Warspite* 'waltzed' to what seemed certain doom with 'her tiller jammed and her guns still firing'. Now, as then, Captain, officers and men united in their determination to get their crippled ship back to port.

It was imperative that we were moved out of there in double quick time. Towing was the only answer. It took a heated discussion, with much bad language, between our Skipper and the 'local' American Admiral before he agreed to allocate us three tugs, one to tow and the others to push us out of trouble. With no lights except battery lamps and no fans or machinery running, the silence that enveloped the ship was eerie as we were towed, at four knots, screened by destroyers, en route to Malta. With no forced ventilation the atmosphere resembled that in a long-submerged submarine. Confucius may have decreed that 'it is better to travel than to arrive', but had he travelled on this journey from Salerno Bay to Malta, he would have developed a quite different philosophy, I am sure.

It was the 16th September, 1943. The weather was hot and the sea calm. At 2 a.m. on the 17th we had come only fifteen miles from Salerno. We were three feet deeper in the water and listing heavily to starboard. There was no sign of Jerry but it was possible that he thought that he had sunk us. In fact Lord Haw Haw claimed that we were sunk. My father had heard him on the wireless (radio) but, thankfully, ignored the announcement as so much of what Haw Haw broadcast was false and designed simply to demoralise. We had no drinking water but survived on a limited supply of lemonade, biscuits and corned beef.

As we passed through the Messina Straits, between Sicily and Italy, Mount Etna seemed to get nearer and nearer as the powerful tide pushed us closer to the Sicilian shore. One of the American tugs detached itself from our stern and, in an almighty effort to stop our drift, she made another dent in the port side to add to that caused by the glider bomb.

All the time, despite the best efforts of the baling party, of which I was one, the list caused by the flooded starboard engine room was getting worse and we were glad to take on board a special engineering officer, Commander Anthony Kimmins, a renowned playwright in civilian life, who advised us as to how best to control it. The pumps were unable to cope with the tons of water slopping around between decks and the only way was to shift it manually – with buckets. Down below decks, fill the bucket, hoist it up to the top deck and over the side with it. All this for hour after hour, in the sub-tropical heat of the Mediterranean. During the night we were joined by two Dido class Cruisers. They took over the tow from the American tugs, which set off on their way back to Salerno Bay. In a way, I was sorry to see them go. The ribald banter that had floated across the hallowed Quarterdeck of the *Warspite* from the crews of the two 'pushers', as they stood with their feet on the guard rail smoking their huge cigars, had been a constant source of comic relief for us.

Transferring the tow from the tugs to the cruisers did not pass without incident, for the towing pennant, a thick, very heavy wire mesh cable, snapped. It was with great fortune that no one was caught by the whiplash and, praise be, no more casualties were added to those already suffered.

As we neared the shores of Sicily and the list to starboard increased despite our laboured efforts, talk increased of the possibility of abandoning ship – not seriously, though to be truthful, not entirely jokingly. The thought of a swim ashore followed by survivors' leave seemed a highly tempting prospect. In reality, however, nothing would have shaken us from our determination to get the 'Old Lady' back to Malta.

It was now that we said 'goodbye' to our ten dead shipmates. They had made the supreme sacrifice and with full Naval Honours, their bodies were consigned to the sea.

At last, after more than four days on a journey that usually takes hours, exhausted from lack of sleep, we sighted that precious island.

The normal routine for a 'big ship' entering harbour is for officers and crew to fall in on the upper deck. In this case it was 'Officers and crew-with-enough-kit fall in on the upper deck'. Many of us had lost everything except the clothes we stood up in when our locker flats were flooded and we mustered in the port hangar – out of sight.

The Captain ordered our Marine band to play *Little Old Lady* as we entered harbour – this, of course, in honour of the dear old *Warspite*. The Marine Band Master regretted that his band did not know *Little Old Lady* but the Captain insisted that they play it anyway.

Imagine the scene as we limped, listing badly, the Officers and 'men-with-clothes' at attention on the upper deck, the Marine band discordantly attempting the tune of *Little Old Lady* and we, in the port hangar, singing what words we knew at the top of our voices. All this accompanied by the sound of welcoming sirens from the ships in the harbour. The 'Old Lady' was back in Malta at last.

The End of the Affair...

As I look through my wartime memories, I find them dominated by one ship – H.M.S. *Warspite*, 'The Old Lady'. I have long understood why ships are called 'she' rather than 'it'. As with all true mariners, mine was a love affair and, as with many love affairs, it was to end.

Back in Malta, in 1943, it was necessary to tow the 'Old Lady' into dry dock to ascertain the full extent of the damage caused by the glider bomb attack. Dry dock

The 15-inch guns of the Warspite belching fire as they hurled shells at the German positions.

usually means shore leave but, in this instance, not for the 'kitless' ones. However, within a week, the lack of appropriate dress for going ashore was remedied as more kit arrived from the U.K. Meanwhile we were to learn that the damage could not be repaired at Malta and we would have to be towed to the larger Gibraltar dock. A skeleton crew was selected, myself among them, and we bade farewell to our friends in Malta. After a painfully slow but unadventurous journey we arrived at 'the gateway to the Mediterranean', a small piece of land inhabited, at that time, almost entirely by sailors. There was not much to do or see and I was glad to receive orders to embark on the troop ship, S.S. *Samaria*, which was homeward bound for the U.K.

This was the last we were to see of 'The Old Lady', although not quite the end of her illustrious and gallant career. Before her guns finally fell silent she was to take part in the bombardment of the Normandy coast in preparation for the D-Day landing. On her way from Portsmouth to Rosyth she hit a mine. This was her final action in a proud career that included Narvik, Taranto, Salerno and Normandy in addition to the other engagements outlined in these memoirs.

After the war, while on the way to be broken up, *Warspite* was driven into Prussia Cove by mountainous seas, became a total wreck, and sank in St Michael's Bay, Cornwall. Visitors to the area can still see her boiler at low tide. The rest of her has been dismantled. Some locals have tables and chairs made from *Warspite* timbers. As the Coxswain of the Mousehole lifeboat said at the time: 'She is where most admirals like to finish their job – buried at sea'. I like to think that she rejected this ignominious death and still guards the waters of our shores. Perhaps the love affair has not yet ended!

CHAPTER SIX

Home and Dry

Normally, sailors do not like travelling on troop ships – not being in charge of their own destiny as it were. In the *Samaria* allocation of messing quarters was fairly regimented – the Army in the bowels of the ship, the Air Force between decks and the Navy above them. Further complications of these arrangements were caused by the presence aboard of contingents of W.R.N.S., W.A.A.F.S. and A.T.S. (Perhaps the S.S. of the ship's name stood for segregation of the sexes. If so, it was poorly named – not with 'Jack' around.)

Because the *Samaria* was not able to visit South Africa to revictual we were short of food and, for the entire trip, we ate almost nothing but corned beef – presented in a variety of ways – but always corned beef. For many years after this I could not face corned beef. Because of this diet many of us suffered from stomach complaints, and were also plagued by mosquitoes. On this ship I learnt to play bridge to pass the time. I haven't played since. I also took part in a Concert Party in which a shipmate and myself recited a monologue entitled 'On the Way to the Old U.K.' in the style of a well known act at that time called the 'Western Brothers'. I also did a solo tap dance, a skill that I acquired at the age of ten. To this day I will tap at the drop of a hat. After a detour via the Azores to avoid enemy subs, it was great to see the lights of Liverpool.

And so it was back to Devonport and home on leave. My family was relieved to see me, after hearing Lord Haw Haw's false news of the *Warspite*'s fate.

The Final Curtain

R.D.F. (Radio Direction Finding), otherwise known as Radar, was a British invention that enabled us to locate and identify enemy aircraft and ships at night and before they could be spotted by the human eye. This shortened the war considerably for the Allies. So little was known about it in the early years that, for example, in 1942, when a Radar Rating in the *Shropshire* was required by the Captain to join Sunday Prayers and the Radar Officer told the Captain that the rating was looking for the Calibration Pip, he was excused. This happened to be a beam of light on the P.P.I. (Planned Position Indicator).

When I got home to England in 1944 things were very different and many courses in the use of Radar were being run. I had undertaken an officer's course at H.M.S. *King Alfred*, which once again I failed, so now I was to go to the Isle of Wight for a ten weeks' course on Radar. I then took another Radar course in Portsmouth, became an R.C.2 and was drafted to the Destroyer *Terpsichore* (Goddess of the Dance and Muses), who certainly lived up to her name in a force eight gale in the Bay of Biscay – the only time in my Naval career when I came close to being sea-sick. We were on our way to join the Americans to be part of the British Pacific Fleet. Churchill had insisted that the British Navy be represented there.

The war in Europe was over. We had all celebrated V.E. Day in London. On the *Terpsichore* I was in charge of the Gunnery Radar with the assistance of the Radar Mechanic. As a measure of my inexperience, I ought to relate that one night I was repeatedly reporting a blip on the P.P.I. (Planned Position Indicator) that appeared to be getting nearer and nearer, when the Captain suggested that I stop reporting it as it was beginning to rain. I had been following a rain cloud!

With ships now able to use the Suez Canal, it was quite an experience visiting Port Said and the unbearably hot Gulf of Aden, then on to Colombo in Ceylon (Sri Lanka) and across the ocean to Freemantle, Australia, the port for Perth. Unfortunately, I was prevented from staying with the *Terpsichore* on her voyages in the Pacific and her eventual attendance at the Japanese surrender in Tokyo Bay. I had developed a medical condition that required surgery.

After I was transferred to the Naval Barracks at Hargraves Park in Sydney, I had an idea that I felt could be a good revenue spinner. I bought a car for £25 with the idea of running a taxi service for naval personnel from the Barracks into Sydney. Unfortunately I never got any further than Sydney Bridge, where the car expired.

In the summer Sydney could be a very hot place. One particular day we were obviously celebrating something special with the help of some Australian brandy we

41

called firewater. The effect of the intense heat was such that I lost one complete day and woke up in a bed at the local pub in Picton, a small suburb of Sydney, being looked after by the landlord's daughter. My companions had managed to start the car and we had got as far as Picton. There we were forced to abandon it in a field. Subsequently we made many trips to this isolated village and even managed to rescue the car, although we had to push it to get into first gear. One of the tyres wore out and we were desperate to replace it. Fortunately my friend Gordon Morren, the son of the Chief Constable of Edinburgh, knew the Premier of New South Wales and, through his influence, we managed to get a tyre. Unfortunately the car expired again shortly afterwards.

One evening we decided to visit the local dance. One of my friends had taken a fancy to one of the barmaids and I, of course, took Daphne, the daughter of the publican. Halfway through the evening my friend disappeared and we found him outside with a broken nose. Apparently his girl friend's boy friend objected to the Navy taking over. As there were no police in this area and we were outnumbered by the Aussie toughs, we felt that discretion was the better part of valour and hurriedly returned to the pub. The story has a happy ending as we sold the car for £25 before we left Australia. We heard afterwards that it had given up the ghost again, this time permanently.

The war with Japan ended with the dropping of the atom bomb on Nagasaki and we celebrated V.J. Day in Sydney. I applied for compassionate leave on the way home to break off my engagement to Elsa, the nurse in

Port Elizabeth. I needn't have bothered – I think Elsa had forgotten me anyway.

I took passage in the Aircraft Carrier *Indomitable* to Cape Town and hitched a lift in a Royal Air Force plane to Port Elizabeth and back. At Cape Town I joined a troop ship back to Devonport Barracks, where, shortly afterwards, I was demobbed. Five years of my life were over. It was back to Finnigan's Department Store in Manchester – but that's another story...

Epilogue

The cost of World War II, both financially and in terms of human suffering, was even greater than that of World War I. The political effects were also more sweeping. Europe lay in ruins. Germany, once the strongest nation in Europe, was occupied by Allied Military Forces. The major European nations were too weak to hold on to their colonies. The United States and the Soviet Union emerged from the war as the world's leading powers. Out of the horrors of two World Wars came attempts to settle disputes peacefully. A new international organisation, the United Nations (U.N.), was established near the end of the war to provide a meeting place where countries could try to work out their political differences.

CHAPTER SEVEN

Learning the Trade

When I travelled from Plymouth for the last time in my government issue, commonly known as a demob. suit, I never realised what changes to my life the next 50 years would bring. I had mixed with every strata of society aboard ship, fighting alongside them and learning to communicate with them. The restrictive barriers of my early life before the war had been stripped away. This was to stand me in good stead for the rest of my life.

After a period of leave, it was a return to Finnigan's department store in Deansgate. I travelled from Altrincham to Manchester and back each day on an electric train and, in between, began to learn the art of merchandising. Finnigans produced travel leather goods, including luggage and small leather goods, and Reuben Farrel, a grandson of Brian Finnigan's partner (see Prologue), headed a team in the Deansgate building as the Salford factory had closed during the War. We also manufactured in premises at Ramillies Street in London. In addition to travel goods, our many departments also included men's wear, ladies' wear, gifts and a sports department, where, under the watchful eye of Tom, our resident professional, I proceeded to improve my golfing skills. I began to learn the trade and was introduced to buying in the gift department.

Because during the War Finnigans had made a good profit producing webbing equipment, they had the choice of paying the Government excess profits tax or spending the money on my training. Brian, my cousin, who was Managing Director, decided that I should go to Switzerland, learn French and experience the retail jewellery and watchmaking trade. Later I would be sent to the U.S.A., where I would join Macys' 'training squad' in New York, probably the finest retail training in the world.

Meanwhile I continued to live at home at Tree Oaks. During the War my father had converted the house into three flats and an upstairs/downstairs section for the family. We no longer needed, nor could we afford, all the servants but continued to employ a cook. Also, from being my governess, Cecile Amor had become Father's housekeeper. Fortunately the said cook did not object to my frequent forays into the kitchen where I tried out my cooking skills, an occupation I enjoy even to this day. Over the years I have often taught my girlfriends to cook, while my sister attended two finishing schools and a cooking course. Obviously the way to a man's – or a lady's – heart is through their stomach.

Swiss Sojourn

It was 1947 and time for me to move on to Switzerland for the first part of my training assignment.

In Geneva my workplace was Vacheron & Constanin,

one of the most elegant jewellers in Switzerland, situated on Tour d'Ile. Vacheron & Constanin sold top-class jewellery, Vacheron & Constanin hand-made watches, and Jaeger le Coultre watches. Jaeger le Coultre was the parent company and both *marques* of watches are sold throughout the world. On my first day, M. Ketterer, the Manager, told the staff: 'Today Mr Finnigan will speak English; from tomorrow, nothing but French.' I was certainly thrown in at the deep end!

They say that the language of love is international and fortunately my girlfriend in Geneva, Janet Fischer, couldn't speak English, making it essential that I improve my French. I soon settled in to life in this wonderfully cosmopolitan city. My father had arranged for me to stay with the Patry family. M. Patry was a doctor and the head of a very large family including a daughter, Thérèse, who was just about my age. There were also at least 70 relations including the grandmother. As well as a comfortable flat in town, they had a summer house on Lac Lemon and we spent many of our weekends 'messing about in boats'. It was great fun to sail across the lake to France and explore the surrounding countryside. It is fashionable in most autobiographies to talk about sexual encounters; as you will have gathered from this narrative, I enjoyed the company of young ladies and I cannot let this period of my life go by without referring to a certain lady (no names, no pack drill) who really enjoyed her sex. On one occasion when we made love she had three orgasms, I seem to remember. We both found this experience highly enjoyable and never referred to it again. After all, I was 24 years of age and she was 30.

Vacheron & Constanin was one of the most prestigious shops in Geneva and the clientèle included many influential and rich people. I particularly remember the Princess de Rethy, widow of the King of the Belgians, who was a regular visitor. I enjoyed practising my French on the customers and, of course, being 'wheeled out' to look after the British and other foreigners who couldn't speak French. One particular day a gentleman from South America came in for a watch. I showed him what I thought was a great bargain and managed to persuade him to part with his money. When I went into the back of the shop, the staff were rubbing their hands – apparently this was a piece of old stock which they had been trying to get rid of for some time. Of course, had I known this, I probably would not have been successful, which just goes to show how much of selling is in the mind. It is a bit like sport, where a positive mental attitude can often make up for a lack of skill.

As with most continental tourist cities, the shopping day was long. We started at 8am and finished at 7pm with two hours for lunch. As it was summer, we were able to swim in the Lake at lunch time, coming back to the shop duly refreshed. I enjoyed talking to the watchmakers, who taught me some of their craft and their argot, which included 'sa gaz' and 'sa masse' (alternative versions of 'ça va', meaning 'all right') as well as introducing me to the intricacies of 'horlogerie' (watchmaking and repairing).

47

It was not until the end of the 1940s that Britain began to recover from the effects of the War, with food still rationed and consumer goods in short supply. It was therefore a pleasure to spend six months in a country that had not been affected. Today it is being claimed that Switzerland benefited considerably from the Jewish funds that were deposited in Swiss Banks during the War. No wonder the Bankers were described as the Gnomes of Zurich. At that time these things were far from my mind as I concentrated on improving my French and my selling skills, meeting charming people and travelling the length and breadth of this delightful country. One of my highlights was a visit to the *Bal des Étudiants* (Students Ball) with Janet Fischer, where the cabaret was headed by the Nicholas Brothers, probably the greatest tap dancers of the day, who featured in many Hollywood films.

All good things have to come to an end and sadly I had to say goodbye to my friends. While serving in the shop I had met a family called Van Hoosear from the U.S.A. and they had invited me to look them up if I ever visited San Francisco. As with most invitations, they never expected to see me again – but in this case they were wrong.

Now that Britain is a part of Europe, I believe that it is even more important for inhabitants of this tight little island to speak another language. Today many people go abroad for their holidays and are often 'conned' by the locals as they are unable to understand a word they say. In 1947 I found it most useful to be able to speak French, the second language of Europe, and I am grateful to Cecile Amor, who was half French and spoke to me at home in French and English. This helped to make my six months in Geneva even more enjoyable. Cecile enjoyed playing Beethoven and Mozart sonatas and duets with her friends. She also played tunes such as Drake's Drum for the family to sing, and she helped me to develop a love of classical music, starting with the romantics such as Beethoven, Liszt, Chopin and Schubert, and eventually, with the help of Mary (my first wife), the classics, particularly Mozart. I took piano lessons and always regretted that I didn't continue, as it is useful to be able to play at a party if asked. As you will gather, music played a great part in my life (excuse the pun!) and my mood is often affected by the music I hear.

Cecile Amor was my ally in the rather heated disagreements I had with Dad. These were probably caused by the generation gap. Eventually, I left home and established my own flat in another part of Bowdon. Today I am often described as the absent-minded professor and the following story will illustrate where I inherited this trait. One morning Dad set out for Manchester in the car and arrived home by train. Cecile said: 'Herbert, didn't you take the car into town?' Dad then returned and two hours later found it where he had parked it.

In the 1940s everything was in short supply, so that it was a great experience for me to find unusual gifts for Finnigans and watch them 'walk out' of the shop to help satisfy the thirst created for 'nice things' during this period of austerity. I also enjoyed meeting our customers, who found Finnigans a great place to shop compared to the hustle and bustle of department stores such as Lewis's or even Kendal Milnes.

CHAPTER EIGHT

American Adventure

In 1949 it was time for me to set out on another Great Adventure, this time across the Atlantic.

Liverpool Docks was not the brightest place from which to embark but it was exciting to board the liner that was to transport me to New York. The conditions were very different from the cramped quarters of the S.S. *Samaria*. The *Media* and her sister ship the *Parthia* were part of the Cunard fleet that included the *Queen Mary* and *Queen Elizabeth*. These regularly travelled from Southampton or Liverpool to New York and to Toronto in Canada. During the age of the Ocean Liner, Cunard had a slogan, *'Getting there is half the fun,'* and if I had the choice today of flying or going by sea, I would certainly choose the latter. But more about this later.

Dad, Pam, Brian Finnigan and his American wife, Pat saw me off and as we quaffed our pre-voyage champagne, Brian gave me two things which I found of great value. The first was a copy of Dale Carnegie's *How to win Friends and Influence People* and the other was a bit of advice as follows: 'No matter what time you go to bed, always be on time for work or meetings in the morning.' I have tried to follow this advice all my life, but have not always succeeded.

Because the *Media* was small and all one-class, it was a

very friendly ship. After the austerity of post-war Britain, it was wonderful to be served good food at all times and to be able to order anything you liked even if it was not on the menu. The service was superb and the seven days seemed to fly by. As with most sea voyages, inhibitions were dropped and after dancing into the early hours I did not always return to an empty cabin. One night I had to sneak out of my lady companion's cabin after 9am, having overslept. I was still in my evening dress – rather embarrassing.

Naturally we organised an entertainment for the ship's passengers, and in spite of the rolling ship, I still managed to tap dance without falling over. As we approached the coast of the U.S.A. the skyline of Manhattan appeared through the morning mist and, whilst steaming up the Hudson River, we were awe-struck by the panorama that stretched before us, with the Empire State Building (at the time the tallest building in the world) towering above the New York skyline. Surely one of the most impressive sights to greet a traveller approaching a country for the first time! This was to be my home for many months to come.

A Wonderful Town

Pat Finnigan's brother Jack, who lived near New York, met me at the docks and guided me to the King George V Hotel, where I was to stay until I found a room closer to Macys. The sheer size of the buildings in New York took my breath away. I'd seen plenty of films that featured views of the city, but they could not prepare me for the on-the-spot experience. New York was an easy place to explore, with all the streets going one way and the avenues intersecting them: Lexington Avenue, Madison Avenue, Park Avenue, Fifth Avenue, 42nd Street – all well-known names from the films – Time Square and 34th Street, the location for R.H. Macy and Company, also the film *Miracle on 34th Street* (featuring Macys' Thanksgiving Day Parade). At one time the store building covered a complete city block except for a small 'Automat' restaurant. Macys offered to purchase this and at first the owners refused. Eventually they succumbed and I imagine that the proprietors became millionaires overnight as a result of the vast sum they had to pay to become the largest store in the world. They were bigger even than the Marshal Fields store in Chicago, where before the War my cousin Brian had spent some time learning the trade and studying branch stores in the suburbs. It was this experience that eventually led to the idea of Finnigans moving to Wilmslow.

Macys' building in Herald Square consisted of 24 storeys, 12 of which were selling floors while the rest comprised stock rooms and two cafeterias for the customers and the staff. It took me more than two weeks to find my way round the store, and even then I got lost on occasions. The 10,000 employees became 20,000 at Christmas – the size of a small town. My fellow members of the Training Squad included young men and women from business schools throughout the U.S.A., including the famous Harvard Business School. They were normally destined for jobs throughout the Macy empire, but some moved on to become executives in other stores such as Bloomingdales, Saks Fifth Avenue or Marshal Fields, or else in other industries. Jack Strauss, President of Macys, had a motto which said: 'if you can merchandise pins, you can merchandise anything'. With the agreement of Jack Strauss I was being paid by Finnigans and it was a wonderful opportunity for me to learn the basics of selling and merchandising and to extol the virtues of Macys when I returned home. Training for the sales assistants was superb – certainly well ahead of any U.K. stores even today and, curiously enough, my first assignment was in the luggage department. Each morning in our first two weeks we attended training class where we were taught the rudiments of selling – from the correct way to approach the customer to closing the sale. We were also taught the history of the Company and how to use the mechanical devices such as the till. Not all of this rubbed off on the staff, but at least they were given the basics.

As well as getting acclimatised to Macys, I had to get used to the city and find myself a place to live, preferably near to the store. I was lucky enough to find a room on the corner of Lexington Avenue and 34th Street, which meant that all I had to do was fall out of bed in the morning and, after a quick breakfast in a drug store – eggs over easy, toast and coffee – be at work in five minutes. It cost me 9 bucks (approximately £2.75) a week and the landlord was an interesting character, who had taught elocution to the sons and daughters of film magnates in Hollywood. He told me that Mr Jack Warner, one of the famous Warner Brothers, had a habit of sneaking into the class. He needed to learn English 'proper'. As a first generation immigrant from Eastern Europe, he found it difficult and didn't want to be shown up by his children.

In 1949, four years after the end of the War, America was not used to visiting 'Brits' and most Americans tended to welcome us with open arms as saviours of civilisation as we know it. I felt that they pictured us standing on the Cliffs of Dover turning back Hitler and his troops. After all, we had stood alone in 1940.

I enjoyed a great reception at Macys and liked talking to the average New Yorker, although, with its cosmopolitan population, it was probably the least friendly city in the U.S.A.

Food, which was certainly a problem in the U.K., was no problem in New York. I managed to sample all types of cooking, and settled for a restaurant in Lexington Avenue called Susan Princes, which featured American food such as Boston Clam Chowder and sported what was called a 'Family Table'. Here I met a variety of young people, most of whom were strangers to the City. They were a mixed bunch, who came not only from the USA, but also from other parts of the world. It was a great way to make friends, particularly with young ladies, some of whom stayed at the Barbizon Hotel for Women in the same street. The rumour was that one young man got above the first floor of the Barbizon and was never seen again. At that time the rules were very strict. I wonder what it is like today?

As executive trainees with Macys we had our activities planned for us and I was able to experience every aspect of store life. For example, in the Stationery

Department, I was put in charge of the back-to-school sales and I am proud to say that we had the best 'back-to-school' period in the history of Macys. Another time, while working in Budget Dresses, I was given a table of dresses on the ground floor to look after – very valuable selling space – with a sales target to reach by 12 noon. I vividly remember having a set-to with a stock boy in the Budget Dress stock room on the 16th floor. I desperately needed stock for my table, but he was having coffee. Unions were so powerful at Macys that no executive was allowed to push a trolley, as he very vividly pointed out. Sadly I did not reach the target and the table was taken away.

I will never forget the first million dollar day at Macys, when the turnover exceeded that sum for the first time. It was a proud moment for all the employees and was celebrated with parties in all departments.

At that time Macys had three branch stores in the New York area, including one that was about to open in Flatbush (i.e. Brooklyn). Three of us were given the job of supervising the opening. On the dot of 9am hundreds of customers streamed in. There were so many people that we had to stop the elevators and make the up escalator go down and the down escalator go up. New Yorkers seemed to thrive on chaos and, despite the great numbers, we managed to serve them all, resulting in another record day for Macys and a triumph for the Training Squad.

Macys was an exciting place to work in, with merchandise of a quality somewhere between Selfridges and John Lewis. Like John Lewis's 'Never Knowingly

Undersold', Macys had slogans, and theirs were as follows: *'Nobody but nobody undersells Macys'* and *'6% less for cash.'* This meant that we competed favourably with all the big stores in New York and, if anybody found anything elsewhere at the same price or less, we guaranteed to sell it at least 6% less. This only applied to stores that gave the same service, such as delivery and did not include cut-price shops such as Kleins or Woolworths.

'Ball Point Pen' wars

An amazing story illustrating Macys policy in action concerned the so called 'ball point pen wars'. Macys first introduced the new biro pen and sold it at 19.99 dollars. Gimbels sold it for 18.99 and eventually Macys ended up buying the pens from Gimbels and selling them for a dollar fifty. Everyone knows the price of ball point pens today.

As executive trainees we spent some time patrolling other stores to try and find items that competed in price with our own and were rewarded for each one we found. We also disguised ourselves as customers and shopped in the store, reporting on the service we received from the selling staff. I always felt that this was hard on the departments concerned but it was all part of Macys' policy of giving the customer the best possible service. It kept staff on their toes as they had no idea when they were likely to receive a visit from a 'spy'.

During my training assignment as a Floor Supervisor, I found the advice in Dale Carnegie's Book to be highly relevant, particularly when dealing with awkward customers.

As my time at Macys covered some of the hottest months of the year (and in August the humidity was unbearable) we often spent our weekends at Jones Beach on Long Island Sound. I had made 'very good friends' with Leila Roig, whose father was a Finance Director of PANAGRA (Pan America Grace Lines), a branch of Pan American Airways. The Roig family lived at Great Neck on Long Island, a suburb of New York, and were great anglophiles, so much so that they even called their house 'Puddleby' after the famous 'Doctor Doolittle' stories. Leila, or Dee Dee as she was called, arranged for her father to take me to an extremely up-market golf club of which he was a member and I remember how impressed I was with the state of the wonderful course facilities provided for the members. After years of austerity, it was like another world. Finnigans' agent in New York was a Southern gentleman called Emory Rylander who came from Americus Georgia. Dee Dee, Emory and I went around together and one day when visiting Jones Beach with a friend of Dee Dee's, who happened to be secretary of the Democratic Party in New York, Emory asked her what she did – knowing perfectly well. On being told, Emory said 'I am a Democrat too, a Jeffersonian Democrat before the communists got in.' This was a great conversation stopper as the young lady concerned didn't say another word to Emory all afternoon. Obviously the Civil War still went on. As well as Dee Dee, I was rather smitten by a young lady from Madison, Wisconsin called D'Alyse, who was on the Macys training

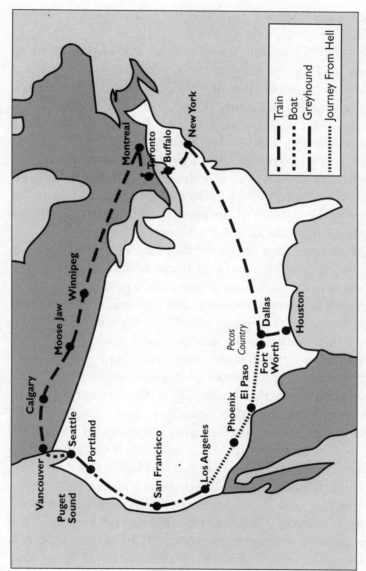

American Trip

squad, and later I travelled to Madison to meet her family.

The six months at Macys flew by. We worked hard all week and played hard at the weekends. As I was a jazz and dance music fan, it was great to dance to such famous bands as Tommy Dorsey and Stan Kenton, often in open air venues such as the Tavern In The Park (Central Park). One of the training squad, Wally Selkirk, lived in Pennsylvania, about two hours away from New York City and we would drive up on Saturday and return on Sunday night after helping him to dam the river at the bottom of his garden and dancing Saturday night away at the local Barn Dance.

After spending six months at Macys, it was time for me to move on, as Dad and Brian had arranged for me to work over Christmas at the Nieman Marcus Store in Dallas. They were customers for Finnigans' luggage and sold more of Finnigans' solid butt hide suitcases than any other outlet in the States. Good leather obviously appealed to the tough Texas ranchers. Mr Stanley Marcus was a good friend of Brian's. At the time Dallas was going through a boom. Oil wells were springing up overnight in people's gardens and Texans were becoming instant millionaires. Nieman Marcus had cashed in on this and had become fashion advisers to these *Nouveaux Riches* Texan Ladies. They stocked designer clothes such as Norman Hartnell and Balmain and it was said that whatever was required they could supply, including 'submarines for him and for her'. This was quite a different environment from Macys, but I really enjoyed it. As an Englishman, I was feted and fussed over. I remember a special party given in my honour in the dress department, surrounded by beautiful Texas Belles, where we sang English songs. Texas had a reputation for the most beautiful women in the U.S.A. and many of these worked for Nieman Marcus in Dallas. These glamorous assistants would sit the lady customers in the changing room and sell them outfits for every period of the day from the skin upwards. Their men appreciated this so much that the store arranged a special night at Christmas for men only where the champagne flowed and glamorous girls modelled scanties and showed off some of the fabulous jewellery. Needless to say, the returns the next day were fairly considerable.

(It is well a known fact that most men buy underwear for their girl friends or wives that *they* like, but this often proves to be impractical and unappreciated.) Many unattached girls were attracted to work at Nieman Marcus and this evening tended to become a marriage market.

The following incident illustrates how seriously Nieman Marcus took their position as advisers to the community. A very rich Texan brought her 12 year-old daughter into the store to buy her a fur coat. The assistant advised that this would not be a wise purchase for such a young girl, as she could be a laughing stock at school. The customer sent for Stanley Marcus. Stanley backed up his sales assistant and the lady stormed out, vowing never to return. She came back five years later, thanked the assistant and Stanley for the advice, and bought a fur coat for her daughter.

While in New York I had made friends with a charming lady whose mother lived in Houston – and it was the old invitation – if you're ever in Houston look up my mother. Once again this came true.

In America this was the age of the train. I had travelled from New York to Dallas by train in great comfort and with superb service and food. In my two and a half years in the States I used the plane only once. I decided to visit Houston immediately after Christmas and when I arrived at the station I discovered that most of the hotels in Houston were full up with conventions, so my taxi driver took me to a strange establishment somewhere out of town. I proceeded to telephone my friend's mother to tell her I had arrived. In the morning I was awakened by a telephone call from my friend, who said that her mother had not slept a wink that night worrying about me sleeping in that dreadful place and that she would collect me and take me to her home. I was a little concerned about the constant comings and goings during the night and now believe I spent the night in a brothel. I had not, of course, utilised the services provided by that establishment.

My hostess was a doctor's wife, Mrs Leadbetter. She and her family lived in a prosperous suburb of Houston called Inwood Park. Her hospitality was overwhelming and she even offered me the use of the Lincoln Continental in the garage. She had a younger daughter and an older son and, because it was the Christmas season, I was invited to every Open House party in the area. I was introduced as 'our English friend' and the whole group of us young people had a great time, including midnight swims in the Gulf of Mexico.

I planned to visit Los Angeles, San Francisco, Portland, Seattle, Vancouver and then back to New York via Toronto and Montreal, calling on the major stores and shops that sold Finnigans' leather goods and, where possible, opening new accounts.

Journey From Hell

At that time in America a system had been introduced by which travellers could move around the country most economically with the help of a travel bureau. For example, if you were driving to Los Angeles from Dallas, you could call in to the local bureau and offer your services as a sort of taxi to anybody who happened to be going your way. Unlike a taxi service, the cost was minimal as the traveller paid only a proportion of the expense involved. The driver would be given a list of travel bureaux on his route where it was possible that other people required the same service. This was a godsend to me as I was on the way to Los Angeles and felt that it could be a great way to see the country.

My nearest travel bureau was in Fort Worth just down the road from Dallas and I was fortunate enough (or so it appeared at the time) to find a U.S. airman who was travelling to L.A. I paid up my 20 dollars and we were on our way. Unfortunately it turned out to be a journey from hell.

The wild country that we were to traverse in Texas was known as the Pecos Territory and in the old West it was administered by Judge Roy Bean. As it was February, the weather was atrocious and as it began to snow, the roads became icy and we very nearly ended up in a snowdrift. We had no chains on the car and to make matters worse, the automatic gear kept slipping which did not help on hills. Our Air Force driver admitted that he did not want to go to L.A. as he was arranging to divorce his wife. He then produced a bottle of whiskey and started swigging it as he drove. When we stopped for a sleep it was so cold that we had to keep the engine running and the heater on and, when we reached Phoenix, Arizona, where we were to pick up another passenger, we were greeted by floods and their first rain for two years. We planned to visit Mexico across the Border at El Paso but were refused entry because it appeared that our driver had gone A.W.O.L. (absent without leave) and my visa expired the next day. Eventually, in spite of not having a valid licence and as our driver became more and more drunk, I was forced to take over the driving. As we crossed the border into California and stopped to have our cars checked for smuggled vegetables or fruit, I clipped another car with our front wing. Fortunately the driver accepted 20 dollars for the damage and we carried on. We had a great laugh at a garage just outside L.A., where we were told quite seriously that we would never get through without chains. Apparently L.A. had not had snow for five years and we found at least two inches on the road. We nearly failed to complete the journey when our driver took over and jumped a red light, avoiding a serious collision by the skin of his teeth. It had taken us

24 hours to travel 1,000 miles and I am convinced that my guardian angel worked overtime. So exhausted was I that, when I checked in at my hotel, I slept for 24 hours and dreamt of disasters avoided.

An Angelic Myth

When Los Angeles became a city in 1850 the population was 1610; in 1997 it had grown to four million. In 1949, when we reached Los Angeles City limits, we still had ten miles of built-up area to traverse before we reached the centre. The name Los Angeles (City of Angels) conjures up a vision of wide boulevards and beautiful buildings. The very reverse was true of the centre. My hotel was surrounded by sleazy shops, night clubs and untidy streets. Suburbs such as Beverly Hills, Pasadena, San Fernando Valley and Hollywood were jewels in the crown. After an adventurous journey by bus to friends in San Fernando Valley – nobody walked and most people had cars – I discovered how the affluent lived. Later I visited Bullocks Wiltshire, the up-market department store that catered for these suburbanites, most of whom were not born in L.A. but had moved there from other parts of the world as well as from the U.S.A. As Bullocks were stockists of Finnigan leather goods, this was a courtesy visit. Our main conversation concerned the weather and, as a visitor, I marvelled that many children had never seen snow before and had to learn to make snowmen and throw snowballs.

Hollywood

Before I left Nieman Marcus, Stanley Marcus had given me an introduction to Bonnie Cashin who had worked for them and was now fashion adviser to 20th Century Fox in Hollywood. She invited me to a day out at the studio. I was lucky to experience the last of the golden years of Hollywood, meet such stars as Ray Milland and see him making a film; to watch Dan Dailey and Anne Baxter dancing on a table for a film musical and to learn that Lassie had a double and that his name was Laddy. I had lunch in the studio canteen and met Buster Keaton, who surely ranks with Charlie Chaplin as the greatest comedian of the silent era. Unfortunately, with the advent of talkies, Buster's usefulness faded but the studio kept him on using him for cameo roles. Sadly he turned to drink and died shortly after my visit. I was also happy to meet one of my favourite glamour girls, Jean Peters, at the studio. I asked her for a date but it was not to be. So near but yet so far. Jean was later to marry Howard Hughes, the famous Director and infamous millionaire recluse.

In 1950 at 27 years of age, Hollywood was, for me, a particularly exciting place to visit. Films had always been an important part of my life and I had actually met some of my boyhood heroes and heroines. I was even asked if I would like to appear on the famous Bing Crosby Radio Show! Unfortunately, as this would have involved money (the idea was to promote Finnigans' Leather Goods) it was not a practical proposition. Another highlight of my visit was to listen to Dizzy

Gillespie, the great trumpeter, then at the height of his fame. I was a proud possessor of many of his records.

I have often been told that I am accident prone and the following story could illustrate this.

In a Strange Town

Sunday is often an awkward day to fill, so I decided to get some sea air and visit Santa Monica, a resort and location that often appears in well-known Hollywood movies. Fairgrounds have always appealed to me with their roundabouts, ghost trains and big dippers and I spotted a small amusement complex on the boardwalk. My gambling instinct led me towards an exhibit that featured the famous 'roll a coin on to numbers and win' (or lose), and I decided to have a go. To my amazement I needed only two more numbers to gain 500 dollars. Then disaster struck and I ran out of cash. I had left my travellers cheques at the hotel, so decided to go and fetch them. When I arrived back at the Fairground, it was getting dark and I was the only punter left. Sadly I started to lose. I felt that I must hit those winning numbers soon, but no luck, and I was beginning to run out of money once again. As I looked round the fairground, the bruisers seem to be coming towards me from all directions, just like a scene from a film such as High Noon. I quickly passed over my money and made a hasty retreat. In hindsight I am convinced that the 'bruisers' had found a way to fix the table while I was away and I did not have a chance. I was stuck in a strange city with no money, which could have been disastrous. Fortunately I managed to borrow money from an English friend who lived in the city, pay my hotel bill, and carry on with the next stage of my journey.

Way Out West

California is the largest state in the U.S. and San Francisco the second largest town in California after Los Angeles. Because I was anxious to see as much of the countryside as possible, I decided to travel by Greyhound – not the racing variety, I hasten to add, but the then famous buses often featured in films. They were very reasonable and comfortable and allowed for stops along the way. I particularly remember the massive Sequoia trees, the world's largest living beings. The General Sherman Tree, a Giant Sequoia in a national park, towers more than 83.8 metres and has a trunk about 11 metres wide. It probably dates from before 200 B.C.

My two favourite cities in the U.S. must be San Francisco and New Orleans. They have a character all their own. During my travels I found that most American cities looked the same and it was often difficult to tell one from the other. San Francisco was different, with its clanging cable cars, fascinating China town and its many hills which give the city a special charm. My hotel was the Mark Hopkins (it must have changed its name by now) on the top of Nob Hill with its superb restaurant, 'Top of the Mark' and its views of the two famous bridges, The Golden Gate Bridge and the Oakland Bridge, which link San Francisco to other parts of the Bay area. Russian Hill rises in the northern part of San Francisco and I was fascinated to learn that it included the crookedest street in the world, a section of Lombard Street which makes eight sharp turns in a city block.

Some two hours' driving time out of San Francisco to the East is the gigantic Sierra Nevada mountain range which stretches all the way up to Vancouver. It is in these mountains, often called the High Sierras, that the people of San Francisco chose to ski. You will recall that I had met members of the Van Hoosear family at Vacheron Constantin in Geneva and had been invited to look them up if I ever visited San Francisco. They could not have been more hospitable and they invited me for a weekend to their ski lodge with their family, which included two attractive young daughters. The weather in San Francisco was relatively mild but when we reached the lodge the temperature was below zero and their lodge was snowed in, which meant we had to do some hand digging before we were able to settle ourselves in to this winter wonderland. I was quite surprised how I managed to descend the miniature mountains without falling over (shades of St Cergue and Auntie Gertie). That weekend made a great break for me and I set off for Vancouver duly refreshed.

Before arriving in Canada I passed through the states of Oregon, which some authorities think was named after the Columbia river (this mighty river was at one time called the Ouragon, which means Hurricane in French) and Washington, named, of course, after

George Washington, the first President of the U.S.A. For this part of the journey I carried on by Greyhound but when I reached Seattle, capital of Washington, I decided to transfer to a boat along the mighty Puget Sound that links Seattle with Victoria and Vancouver Island. Unfortunately I missed the magnificent scenery along the way as a storm came up and blocked the view. I spent a few hours in Victoria, which was even more English than England, finally arriving in Vancouver.

As well as Bullocks Wiltshire in Los Angeles I had visited the Finnigans' stockist in San Francisco, I. Magnin, now part of the Macy group, and stores in Seattle and Portland which I hoped would stock our leathergoods. Whether they bought or not, I was spreading the gospel and hopefully doing a good P.R. job for Finnigans.

CHAPTER NINE

Canadian Capers

I had travelled more than 4,000 miles from New York and now I was in another country, Canada. Vancouver, the largest city in British Columbia, had been colonised mainly by English and Scots and was very British. After the war many Asian immigrants travelled to this part of North America to get away from the troubles in their own countries and some of them used Vancouver as a stepping stone into the U.S.A. As a British citizen I did not need a visa to enter Canada but I certainly needed one to get back to the U.S. As I mentioned earlier, mine had expired and I therefore had to apply for a new one. I should have done this in L.A. or San Francisco but had forgotten all about it in the excitement of the trip. Now I was in trouble as the emigration officials were suspicious about my motives for returning to the States. They even thought that I could be an illegal immigrant and I could see myself either having to go back to the U.K. or being stuck in Canada for weeks. I obviously needed to reach New York as soon as possible. Then I had a brainwave. My cousin Brian had given me an introduction to the British Trade Adviser in Vancouver who was a friend of his. I called on him and explained my predicament. Fortunately his office was in the same building as that of the emigration people and he knew them well. It took him an hour to persuade his friend to let me have a visa and after heaving a gigantic sigh of relief I was on my way.

Vancouver is the railway centre of Canada and at that time the privately owned Canadian Pacific Railway (now known as C.P.L.) took passengers across from the West to the East. Now only special excursion trains make the trip. The railroad across the Canadian Rockies must rank as one of the wonders of the North American continent. The views of the snow-capped mountains and the myriad lakes made the journey a highlight of my trip. The food and the service on the train did not compare with the American experience but the scenery made up for that. When I reached Moose Jaw on the border of Canada and the U.S. it was so cold that my nose froze. The people on the station told me that they had had a mild winter. I wonder what a cold one would have been like! I arrived in Toronto on a Sunday and was greeted by a family I had met on the boat coming over. I was immediately invited to spend the day with them. Fifty years ago, on a Sunday, Toronto was like a ghost town and, on asking where everybody was, I was jokingly told: 'The Catholics are in church, the Protestants in bed and the Jews in Florida.' As it happened, I had a most entertaining day. After lunch Dad and Mum went out and I was invited by the attractive young daughter of the house to spend the afternoon in her bed. I accepted readily, being a red blooded, 27-year-old male. My next stop was Montreal, a bilingual city where I could practice my French. The best side of the Border to view the glories of the magnificent

Niagara Falls was the U.S. side, so I stopped in Buffalo in New York State and sat sipping my drink at one of the only revolving bars in the world and waited for the Falls to come into view. In Hollywood films many screen journeys end at Grand Central Station in New York, so it was appropriate that mine should finish there. My trip of a lifetime had taken 6 months, covering more than 4,500 miles, 16 States and 6 Canadian provinces. I had called on numerous retailers and opened up new outlets for Finnigans and Brian and my father were pleased with my efforts. So much so that they decided to provide me with a station wagon so that I could transport luggage on another trip down through the centre of the U.S. by road.

The highlights of my sales trip by road from New York to New Orleans and back included a day at the races in New Orleans, oysters Rockefeller at Antoine's, (the restaurant featured by Frances Parkinson Keys in her book, *Dinner at Antoine's*) and listening to, and meeting Sharkey Barnardo, the only jazz bugle player in the world. I visited such towns as Louisville (Kentucky), Atlanta, the home of *Gone With the Wind* and the famous Masters' Golf Tournament, and many more.

On returning to New York it was nearly time to go home. I was extremely sorry. The last two years had been a great experience and I was eternally grateful to Finnigans for making it possible. Dee Dee and I were very close, but that is another story. I was on the way home on another small ship. Naturally I had fun before arriving at a rain-swept Liverpool.

Because I have had to rely on long term memory for

this 'sort of autobiography', I am including only highlights and my recollections from fifty years ago. The post-war years were certainly a wonderful time for an Englishman to visit the New World and it was fascinating to study American politics at close hand. On asking the difference between the Democratic party and the Republicans, I was told that they were in and we were out. I learnt that in Texas, despite calling themselves Democrats (Jeffersonian Democrats that is), the businessmen of Dallas acknowledged the King of England rather than Harry Truman, the Democrat President in 1950.

A Republican Senator called Joseph McCarthy carried out a witch hunt against the State Department, claiming that they were dominated by communists, and he and his investigation committee seemed to have taken over the screens of our T.V. sets. His victims included lawyers, librarians, actors and playwrights. Many careers were ruined, including those of famous Hollywood actors and directors. In 1954 McCarthy was censured by the Senate and the age of McCarthyism was over.

As you will have gathered from this narrative, my two years in the States made an indelible impression on my life. I had travelled exclusively in a country that I might never have seen, taken part in potentially dangerous incidents, met a cross-section of people and begun to learn the rudiments of my trade. I was eternally grateful to Finnigans for this opportunity. Now it was back to Deansgate and my family.

CHAPTER TEN

Back to the U.K.

The 1950s

What sort of Britain did I return to in 1950, five years after the end of World War II? King George VI was still on the throne, Princess Elizabeth had married her Greek Prince in 1947 and the Labour Government under Clement Attlee, which had been voted into power in 1945, was running out of steam and would shortly be replaced by a Conservative Government under the wartime leader, Winston Churchill. Although the Labour Government had struggled to restore the economy, rationing and other wartime controls still remained and the Government continued to borrow heavily from the United States. Britain had become a Welfare State with a National Health Service that promised to look after us from the cradle to the grave, a promise that they regret today after fifty years with a rapidly ageing population and not enough money in the state coffers to support them.

Fortunately for Finnigans, many more consumer goods were reaching the market and, after the austerity conditions of wartime Britain, there was a great hunger for so-called luxury goods as they became available. After my stimulating time in America, I was anxious to try out new ideas at Finnigans and, as Sales Manager under Brian Finnigan, I had ample opportunity. Although we had closed our factory in Salford, we still manufactured luggage and small leather goods in the Deansgate building and in Ramillies St., London. With the growing popularity of air travel, cases needed to be lighter and other materials such as nylon had also to be used.

Because of our U.S. connections and the popularity of our luggage and small leather goods with the Americans, Brian and I decided to investigate the market in the U.S. Air Force camps such as Lakenheath and Mildenhall in Suffolk. At that time the Cold War was at its height and the U.S. Air Force was at full alert in Britain, with many of their personnel and families living either in or near the bases. Therefore the Post Exchanges were busy places and proved to be a thriving market for Finnigans. Brian and I enjoyed visiting the bases and sampling the large juicy steaks which were in such short supply in the civilian world. The American airmen and their families welcomed us and obviously appreciated the gifts that we were able to offer them for their shops. Since then most bases have been closed but Fairford, in Gloucestershire, still continues to be used by the U.S.A.F. and was a 'stepping off place' for the recent bombing of Yugoslavia.

As Britain became more prosperous and recovered from the effects of seven years of war, well-known names began to appear on the market. Where hitherto we had been able only to sell so-called luxury goods second-hand, gradually new factories and manufacturing plants began to spring up and we were offered Wedgwood (china and pottery) Lalique (glass from France), Georg Jensen (silver from Denmark) and many other brands of goods from other makers. The wealthy Mancunians, who had made their money before the War through cotton and allied industries, came to Finnigans to find quality. Just as Nieman Marcus in Dallas had served the Nouveau Riche Texans, Finnigans looked after the rich Mancunians.

Top Tennis

My cousin Brian, while at Oxford, had become one of the top tennis players in Britain and had been lucky enough to play with some of the up-and-coming U.S. players during his stay in the States prior to the War. It was natural, therefore, that when Finnigans was given the task of organising the Northern Lawn Tennis Tournament, one of the most important tournaments prior to Wimbledon, he should invite some of his American friends.

These days it is impossible to attract top tennis players without paying them vast sums of money. In the 1950s all tennis was an amateur sport and tournaments were not allowed to pay their players. They could pay their expenses, which were often topped up to attract the best. These players were often referred to as 'shamateurs'. In the years that Finnigans ran the Tournament, we attracted most of the top players of the day, including Doris Hart, Louise Brough and Maureen Connolly (known as Little Mo), as well as Lew Hoad, Ken Rosewall and many more. With such stars, it was not surprising that the tournament was a great success and we enjoyed entertaining the players at the end of the week. It seems to me that there was a greater feeling of comradeship at that time than today when the players are earning so much money. The rivalry was there but many of them played just for the love of the game. Finnigans benefited considerably from the publicity generated and we all enjoyed socialising with them. I had the pleasure of dating Little Mo, with the permission of Teach Tennant, her formidable coach. I took her to Mere Country Club where the manager and the members gave her a great welcome. Maureen was the youngest lady to win Wimbledon at that time. She was only 16 and she won Wimbledon three times. Her untimely death from cancer, at the age of 34, foreshortened a career that could have continued for many years. Another highlight for me was a visit to Wimbledon with Louise Brough as her guest in the players' stand. On June 2nd, 1953 Elizabeth was crowned and we managed to arrange for many of the players, including Doris Hart and Louise Brough, to watch the Coronation procession from a balcony on the Strand. This day was not only close to the anniversary of D Day (the invasion of Europe), but it was also a milestone for British achievement with the conquering of Everest, the world's highest mountain, by Edmund Hilary (now Sir Edmund) and Sherpa Tensing.

As I write this volume on my life much controversy has arisen concerning the so called Millennium Dome which is being built in Greenwich. I believe that it will attract millions of visitors, just as the Festival of Britain did in 1951 and the Great Exhibition of 1851, where arts and manufactured goods from Britain and around the world were featured. Finnigans hand-crafted leather goods, including trunks and suitcases, won a gold medal for quality there. One hundred years later quality was still the policy of the company in all the merchandise we sold. My great-grandfather would have been proud of us.

While in America you will recall that I met and rather fancied Leila Roig, otherwise known as Dee Dee, whose father was President of Pan American Grace Line. Dee Dee and her parents had visited me in Cheshire and I was determined to take a quick trip to New York to talk to her about the future of our relationship and indeed whether it had a future. Air travel was just beginning to become popular so it was with some excitement that I boarded the Pan American Strato Cruiser at Northolt Airport in the days before Heathrow was built.

Encounter

In the 1950s a journey across the Atlantic was liable to be an adventure. Picture a two-storey hotel with wings, seats on the ground floor and a bar and bunks up above. Because it was a so-called luxury flight, the ladies were presented with an orchid and the men with a pair of dark glasses. It was an extraordinary gift. Perhaps they were intended to rest our eyes as we attempted to sleep. I found a large brandy from the bar rather more helpful and I woke up as the plane was preparing to land at Goose Bay in Labrador.

Sarah Churchill. (Courtesy of Camera Club.)

80

As we travelled across the snow and ice in the Airport bus and reached a restaurant surrounded by fir trees, I was reminded of Santa Claus, although I am sure he would not have approved of the breakfast menu – reindeer steak! After we had all been fuelled and watered, including the aircraft, we set off on what we thought would be the final stage of the journey.

I had just dropped off into a fitful doze when I was awakened by a mass movement of passengers to the port side of the plane. Apparently one of the four engines had caught fire and the crew were in the process of putting out the flames with the help of the automatic sprinklers. We were able to view this through the porthole. We were then informed by the captain that there was no danger as we could fly on three engines but as we had not reached the point of no return – an ominous phrase – we would have to go back to Goose Bay.

This time, in the bus on the way to the restaurant, I sat next to an attractive young lady whose face seemed vaguely familiar and, not being backward at coming forward, I began to chat with her about our adventure. As we tucked in to yet more reindeer steak it turned out that this was indeed Sarah Churchill. We laughed about our experience and joked about catching the engine as it fell. Sarah talked about her love of the stage and her relationship with her family and, in the few hours that we had to wait for the arrival of another plane to take us on to New York, I learnt much about this charming and bright-eyed girl. She had already had her share of tragedy with her marriage to, and subsequent divorce from, the famous comedian, Vic Oliver. At that time there did not seem to be any hint of the even more tragic events that were to come. These included the suicide of Tony Beauchamp, her second husband, the death of her third husband, Lord Audley, an alcoholic, and her early death also through alcoholism. It seems unfair that she should have had so much sorrow in her life. As I watched Sarah dancing with Fred Astaire in the film *Royal Wedding* on television, it took me back to Goose Bay in 1953 and the realisation that, without this adventurous journey, I would not have had the privilege of meeting Winston's favourite daughter.

It was good to see New York again and to spend time with Dee Dee, a bright intelligent girl, who had become a great friend but not a partner for life. This was the second time I had revisited a foreign country where I said farewell to a former love. The first was South Africa in 1945. I was now eight years older and probably not a lot wiser. Dee Dee and I managed to visit Sarah's smart Duplex Apartment, which she shared with her husband, Tony Beauchamp, though he was out of town at the time. I was to meet Sarah again in England under different circumstances.

Because petrol was still rationed in the early fifties, it was often necessary to share cars and, on a Saturday night, a group of us used to go out with the idea of getting as drunk as possible. Fortunately there were very few cars on the road and not many policemen and no such thing as the breathalyser. The truth is that we had all come out of the services and were sowing our wild oats, grateful for surviving the War. One evening ten of us shared a sports car with two seats in the front and two occasional seats in the back. On another occasion, after staying the night at a friend's house, I woke up to the sight of my car perched up in the top of the tallest tree in the garden.

I had many girl friends and no less than five engagements (close encounters) but managed to stay single until 1958. My three favourite pastimes in those days were eating, dancing and sex, not necessarily in that order.

As a young man about town, I enjoyed life socially to the full and I was also associated with one of the most highly respected businesses in the North. Later I was to suffer from my newsworthiness but at that time I rather enjoyed it.

I was a member of Mere Golf and Country Club at Bucklow Hill and Brian and I used to play golf there when we had the time. We often danced in the evening. On his visits to Manchester for the panto Vic Oliver, the famous comedian (Hi Gang), who was a friend of Brian's and a very keen golfer (and who, coincidentally, had also been married to Sarah Churchill) would often join us on the golf course. Vic would play in any weather, and on one occasion, after one of the wettest games I have ever played, I ended up with a dose of flu. Every year Vic invited Brian, Pat and me to the Pantomime Ball where I had the pleasure of meeting June, his adopted daughter, who became the next love of my life. I remember June with great affection and our weekends together at my flat in Bowdon. Vic also introduced Freddie Valentine, my best friend, to Olivia

Dale, one of the dancers in the show and they often joined us for the weekends. My cooking speciality consisted of stews powered by a stock pot that I continued to top up as needed.

The Passing of a Friend

One day I unexpectedly met Sarah Churchill at Manchester Airport, on her way to the Television Studios to help with a series on her father's life. We talked about our exciting journey across the Atlantic. We were to meet again very soon.

Apparently the Ideal Home Exhibition in Manchester invited celebrities to open the show, and that year they invited Sarah and Richard Dimbleby. After her appearance with Fred Astaire in *Royal Wedding*, Sarah had become quite famous. Unfortunately her visit to Manchester almost ended in disaster. I had met her the night before the opening and we agreed that I would pick her up the next day at the Midland Hotel where she was staying. Unfortunately Sarah refused to leave her room. She was obviously suffering from a bad case of pre-show nerves combined with a hangover from the night before. Eventually I managed to persuade her to appear and the opening was a great success. At that time Sarah was on the way to becoming an alcoholic. Twenty years later I spoke to her on the phone and she did not recognise my voice. A month later I heard that she had died. A tragic end for a really lovely lady.

A Talent to Amuse

Earlier in this narrative I referred to the genius of Noel Coward and how much he was appreciated when he visited the *Warspite* in Malta. As I write I realise that this year, 1999 is also the centenary of his birth. I have just returned from a performance of *Mad About the Boy*, a Noel Coward anthology performed at the Pump Room, Bath by an amateur group called Serendipity. It was interesting to observe that a new connotation has been placed on certain of his lyrics since he was 'outed' by the public in recent years. 'Mad About the Boy' and 'Chase Me Charlie' have taken on a different meaning. However, whatever his sexual proclivities might have been, there is no performer who has managed to appeal so much to two generations of theatre goers by providing them with such a diet of wonderful melodies and brilliant lyrics. Noel chose Manchester to launch his new shows because he was a believer in the old adage, 'What Manchester thinks today, London thinks tomorrow'. We Mancunians were certainly a hard audience to please and if we liked the particular show, it usually succeeded in the Capital. The Palace Theatre in Manchester saw many great Coward premières and I particularly remember *This Year of Grace*, *Cavalcade*, and *Private Lives*. In the words of 'If Love Were All', from surely his greatest musical tour de force, *Bitter Sweet*, Noel had 'a talent to amuse'. I will never forget Malta. I fear that we shall not see his like again.

This was a period of consolidation for Finnigans. The Bond Street shop in London continued to progress under the watchful eye of my Uncle Bernard. At Deansgate, Brian and I knew that we had to attract more customers as we were already beginning to feel the effects of the lack of parking facilities in the centre of Manchester. It is said that the way to a man's or woman's heart is through their stomach – witness the number of good food restaurants that were springing up all over Britain. We had found an exceptional one in Prestbury called Mathew's, run by a temperamental gay chef who served the most wonderful food. However, if he took a dislike to you, he refused to serve you. Our restaurant in the Deansgate store was not exactly renowned for its good food, though it had managed to tempt the ladies and sometimes the men, to linger over lunch or tea or even coffee and watch the attractive models displaying the latest fashions. Needless to say the men stayed a little longer when these included frilly underwear. The question was: how could we capitalize on this and attract more customers to the shop so that they would spend more money? Fortunately we solved the problem fairly quickly. We found a new Manager, Greg Taylor, late of the American Air Force Base at Burtonwood, and he brought with him Misché, a Frenchman, late of the Savoy in London. Suddenly our food was transformed; Normandie cooking *par excellence*. Wonderful soups served up in those fascinating tureens, Chicken Normande (one of our specialities), pot au feu and many more delicacies, including mouth-watering sweets. The customers flocked in but it was not to last. Sadly we had to part company with Misché as his language and kitchen habits meant that we could not keep kitchen staff and when, one day, Greg Taylor was hit by a flying saucepan, Misché had to go. To this day I will always remember his delectable cooking. He certainly attracted the customers and we never managed to find anybody quite like him. Our Restaurant became the 'Normandie Room' and we even managed to open in the evenings. We continued to serve good food, another love of my life, and our reputation spread throughout the North.

These memoirs seem to be dominated by my love affairs either with members of the opposite sex, such as Elsa in South Africa and Dee Dee in the States, or with inanimate objects such as H.M.S. *Warspite* (the Old Lady). In the 1950s I must include a motor car, my Jaguar XK120, described as a legend in its own lifetime, created 13 years earlier than the famous E. Type and designed by the founder of Jaguar, Sir William Lyons. I feel myself privileged to have owned one of the most exciting sports cars ever built. It lived up to its name when I managed to reach 120 m.p.h. on a memorable journey from Bowdon to Mere along the Chester Road. It should be remembered that this was many years before the first motorway was built. The first X.K. was exhibited at the 1948 Motor Show and the most famous model, the N.U.B. 120, which won the R.A.C. and Alpine Rallies outright for two years running, was still going strong in the anniversary year of 1998. My car was light blue and exciting, and in the language of the young, certainly 'pulled the birds'.

A Good Move

Because the lease was soon due to expire on the building in Deansgate, we would need to find an alternative site. Then fate played into our hands. Brian and I decided to have a drive around the Wilmslow area, an affluent suburb from which many of our customers hailed. Then suddenly we spotted a notice which was to change our lives. Norwich Union Assurance Company was developing a site for several shops in the middle of Wilmslow and was asking interested businesses to apply. I think we both had the same idea: 'Why don't we approach them and suggest that we take the whole site, perhaps subletting any part of it we do not use ourselves?' Thus Finnigans of Wilmslow was born and we were responsible for developing what was probably one of the first out-of-town shopping centres in the country. I personally was sad to be leaving Deansgate but, realistically, parking was difficult and our end of the street became less popular. We decided to keep a foothold in the city so we found a small shop in King Street. This proved not to be satisfactory, so we closed it and moved everything to Wilmslow. We sublet part of the site to Robinson and Cleaver, who specialised in linens, and Coopers, the speciality food people. Eventually we took over their area and Finnigans had the whole building. Because the Normandie Room Restaurant in Deansgate had been such a success we were determined to open a restaurant which could be used in the day and in the evening. This we called the Whaler Room after the founder, Brian

Finnigan, the whaling Captain. The move to Wilmslow proved to be popular with most of our customers. Those living on the other side of Manchester did not appreciate it so much but we were able to provide plenty of parking space and I believe, if it hadn't been for money problems, it could have been a great success. Unfortunately we were under-capitalised and had trouble with the bank and our creditors. In hindsight I believe that we might have found an investor to help us make use of the goodwill that we had built up over the years. We still had a foothold in London and a manufacturing base there (in Ramillies St.). Finnigans' leather was still respected throughout the world although, with the popularity of air travel, new lightweight fabrics were being developed for suitcases which obviously affected the sales of our own handmade leather luggage.

Instead we sold the complete business to an affluent T.V. retailer. My cousin Brian was offered a job in the Cayman Islands and I joined a P.R. company in London. I was proud that Finnigans had provided a great service to the local community over the years, and had been a pioneer in out-of-town shopping. The door had opened but it was shortly to close after the failure of my marriage, and to reopen later with my change of career at fifty. The story of how life continued for me after Finnigans' has still to be told.

Finnigan Family Tree

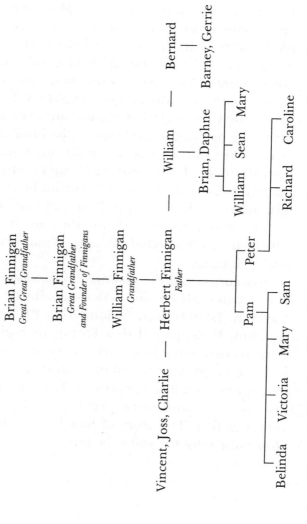

Brian Finnigan
Great Great Grandfather

Brian Finnigan
Great Grandfather
and Founder of Finnigans

William Finnigan
Grandfather

Vincent, Joss, Charlie — Herbert Finnigan — William — Bernard
Father

Pam   Peter   Brian, Daphne   Barney, Gerrie

Belinda   Victoria   Mary   Sam   William   Sean   Mary   Richard   Caroline

Glossary of Naval Terms

Andrew	Navy
Matelot	Sailor
Pongo	Soldier
Square Rig	Sailor's Uniform
Fore and Aft	Officer's and Non-Commissioned Officer's Uniform
Mess Deck	The space where sailors eat and sleep
Ward Room	Officers' dining and meeting room
Forecastle	Front deck
Quarterdeck	Rear deck of ship, commonly known as 'after deck' on some ships
Picket boat	Motorboat used for transporting crew to shore or to other ships. Also for special assignments such as Boom Patrol (see p. 21)
R.C.2 & 3	Radar Control Rating 2nd Class and 3rd Class
W.R.N.S.	Women's Royal Naval Service
Jerry	Germans
Lord Haw Haw	William Joyce, who, during the War, broadcast anti-British propaganda from Germany. His information was often untrue and based on rumour. He was executed as a traitor after the War.

Note: Shore establishments were also designated as 'ships', for example, H.M.S. *Raleigh* at Torpoint, which is still being used as a training centre for sailors. H.M.S. *King Alfred* in Hove and (during the War) H.M.S. *Good Hope* (Seaview Hotel) in Port Elizabeth, South Africa, were used as training centres for potential officers.

Bibliography

Wartime memoirs from *An Able Seamans War*.
Naval pictures from the Archives of the Imperial War
Museum Picture Library.
Original publication of *An Able Seamans War*, Typset
Direct, Bloomfield Road, Bath.